GOODFOOD
Meals In MINUTES

BBC GoodFood

Meals In MINUTES

ORLA BRODERICK

BBC BOOKS

Also published by BBC Books:
BBC Good Food Secrets of Success

Published by BBC Books,
a division of BBC Worldwide Publishing,
BBC Worldwide Limited,
Woodlands, 80 Wood Lane
London W12 0TT

First published 1995
© BBC GOOD FOOD 1995

ISBN 0 563 37125 0

Nutrition notes: Wendy Doyle

Set in Franklin Gothic by Ace Filmsetting Ltd, Frome
Printed and bound in Great Britain by Butler & Tanner Ltd, Frome
Colour separation by Goodfellow & Egan Ltd, Cambridge
Papercase printed by Lawrence Allen, Weston-super-Mare

CONTENTS

INTRODUCTION

BBC Good Food Meals in Minutes has proved to be extremely popular with our readers. Prepared with the busy cook in mind this book contains a selection of quick-to-prepare recipes for starters, main courses, snacks and desserts which make the most of store-cupboard ingredients or ingredients that can easily be bought from the corner shop. Each recipe has the total time it takes to prepare and cook the dish, which is never more than 40 minutes, as well as an indication of its cost. For starters and desserts, recipes under £2 for four people are classed as 'budget', under £3 as 'cheap' and over £3 as 'average'. For main courses and snacks, recipes costing less than £3 for four people are classed as 'budget', less than £4 as 'cheap' and over £4 as 'average'.

For the health-conscious reader, each recipe includes nutrition notes listing the number of calories, and the level of fat, saturated fat, protein, fibre and sodium as 'low', 'medium' or 'high'. These categories are based on guidelines from the Coronary Prevention Group. For both fat and protein, a balanced diet means eating a combination of foods that result in an overall 'medium'. Saturated fat consumption, though, should be 'low'; as far as sodium (salt) is concerned, aim for 'low' intake; as for fibre, optimum intake is 'medium' to 'high'. Many recipes also include variations for the reader to try out.

All the recipes have been developed by senior food writer Orla Broderick and the Good Food team, and have passed our taste tests before going into the magazine and then this book. When you're looking for something quick, tasty and satisfying to eat, try *Meals in Minutes*; in three or four simple steps you'll have a tasty meal in absolutely no time at all.

Mitzie

Mitzie Wilson
Editor-in-chief BBC Good Food

Carrot and cumin potage

- **Total time: 30 minutes**
- **Budget ● Serves 4**

2 tablespoons olive oil
1 large onion, chopped
2 garlic cloves, crushed
2 teaspoons cumin seeds
450 g/1 lb carrots, sliced
1 large potato, chopped
1.2 litres/2 pints vegetable or chicken stock
400 g/14 oz can cannellini or haricot beans, drained
seasoning
natural yogurt, to serve
chopped fresh parsley, to garnish

1 Heat the oil in a pan and fry the onion until softened, then add the garlic, cumin seeds, carrots and potato and cook gently, stirring until the carrots and potato begin to soften.

2 Add the stock and seasoning and bring to the boil; cover and simmer for 15 minutes. Leave to cool slightly, then sieve or purée in a food processor.

3 Return to the pan, stir in the beans and simmer gently until heated through. Transfer to serving bowls, swirl in the yogurt and garnish with parsley.

● *Per serving: calories 253, fat medium, saturated fat medium, protein medium, fibre high, sodium medium*

Goat's cheese toasts

- **Total time: 20 minutes**
- **Average** ● **Serves 4**

½ **thick baguette**

25 g/1 oz butter, softened

100 g/4 oz firm goat's cheese

½ **head of frisée or curly endive, broken into leaves**

2 tablespoons walnut pieces

1 teaspoon crushed peppercorns

FOR THE DRESSING

3 tablespoons walnut or olive oil

1 tablespoon white wine vinegar

pinch of caster sugar

1 teaspoon Dijon mustard

seasoning

❶ Preheat the oven to 180°C/350°F/Gas 4. Cut the baguette diagonally into four large 2.5 cm/1 in thick slices.

❷ Butter the bread on both sides. Cut the goat's cheese into eight slices and top each piece of bread with two slices of cheese, slightly overlapping.

❸ Place on a baking sheet and bake for 10–15 minutes until the cheese is bubbling.

❹ Make the dressing: place the oil, vinegar, sugar, mustard and seasoning in a screw-topped jar and shake until well mixed.

❺ Mix the frisée and walnuts, pour over the dressing and toss to coat. Divide among four plates and top with the toasts. Scatter over the peppercorns.

● *Per serving: calories 539, fat medium, saturated fat medium, protein medium, fibre medium, sodium medium*

Melon, bacon and cucumber salad

- Total time: 25 minutes
- Average ● Serves 4

½ **large cucumber**
1 teaspoon salt
1 small cantaloupe or charentais melon
1 tablespoon olive oil
100 g/4 oz lean bacon rashers, cut into short strips
FOR THE DRESSING
3 tablespoons olive oil
1 tablespoon white wine vinegar
seasoning
handful of fresh mint sprigs, to garnish

❶ Using a vegetable peeler, remove strips of peel from the cucumber to produce a striped effect. Slice into thin rounds. Place in a colander set over a plate and sprinkle with the salt.

❷ Halve the cantaloupe or charentais melon and scoop out the seeds. Using a melon baller, scoop the flesh into balls and place in a salad bowl.

❸ Heat the oil in a small frying pan and fry the bacon until crisp; drain on kitchen paper. Rinse the cucumber slices in cold water and pat dry. Stir into the salad bowl with the bacon.

❹ Place the oil, vinegar and seasoning in a screw-topped jar and shake until blended, then drizzle over the salad. Garnish with mint.

● *Per serving: calories 216, fat high, saturated fat medium, protein medium, fibre medium, sodium high*

Tomato and basil filo

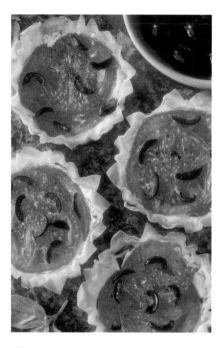

- **Total time: 40 minutes**
- **Cheap ● Serves 4**

150 g/5 oz filo pastry, thawed if frozen
butter, for greasing
50 g/2 oz butter, melted
200 g/7 oz Greek strained yogurt
handful of fresh basil leaves, roughly shredded
2 beefsteak tomatoes, thinly sliced
50 g/2 oz black olives, shredded
seasoning

① Preheat the oven to 200°C/400°F/Gas 6. Using a sharp knife, carefully cut the filo pastry into twelve 10 cm/4 in squares.

② Lightly grease four 10 cm/4 in round flan tins. Use one square of filo to line each tin and brush with a little of the melted butter. Repeat process two more times, using no more than half of the butter, rotating each square as you go to create a jagged edge.

③ Divide the yogurt among the cases, scatter over the basil and seasoning. Cover with tomato and olives; brush the remaining butter on top. Season.

④ Scrunch the edges of the pastry to create a frilled edge. Place the tins on a baking sheet and bake for 15–20 minutes until golden. Serve warm or cold.

● *Per serving: calories 304, fat high, saturated fat high, protein medium, fibre medium, sodium medium*

Chilled leek and potato soup

- Total time: 40 minutes
- Cheap ● Serves 4

25 g/1 oz butter

3 large leeks, sliced

225 g/8 oz potatoes, peeled and diced

600 ml/1 pint chicken or vegetable stock

225 g/8 oz Greek strained yogurt

seasoning

2 tablespoons snipped fresh chives, to garnish

① Melt the butter in a pan, then add the leeks and fry gently for about 5 minutes without browning. Add the potatoes, stock and seasoning. Bring to the boil, cover and simmer for about 20 minutes or until tender.

② Allow the soup to cool slightly, then sieve or whizz in a food processor until smooth. Transfer to a large bowl, cover and chill thoroughly.

③ To serve, stir most of the yogurt into the soup. Adjust the seasoning, spoon a dollop of the remaining yogurt into each bowl and sprinkle with the chives.

● *Per serving: calories 130, fat high, saturated fat high, protein medium, fibre high, sodium high*

Pinwheels of smoked trout

● Total time: 20 minutes
● Average ● Serves 4

100 g/4 oz curd cheese
2 teaspoons finely chopped cucumber
1 tablespoon snipped fresh chives
freshly ground black pepper
100 g/4 oz packet smoked trout slices
½ small cucumber, cut into matchsticks, to serve
mixed salad leaves and lemon wedges, to serve

① Mix together the curd cheese, chopped cucumber, half of the chives and a little pepper in a small bowl. Reserve four of the best slices of trout. Finely chop the remainder and add to the cheese mixture.

② Lay the slices of trout on a work surface. Divide the curd cheese mixture into four and spread a quarter over each slice. Carefully roll up the trout as if you were making a Swiss roll, then neatly trim off the ends and slice each roll into three evenly sized pieces.

③ Arrange on serving plates and garnish with a sprinkling of black pepper and the remaining chives. Serve with cucumber sticks, salad and lemon wedges.

● *Per serving: calories 62, fat medium, saturated fat low, protein high, fibre low, sodium medium*

Onion fritters with chilli sauce

- ● Total time: 25 minutes
- ● Average ● Serves 4

| 100 g/4 oz gram (besan) flour or plain flour |
| 2 teaspoons baking powder |
| 1 teaspoon chilli powder |
| 2 eggs, beaten |
| 4 onions, thinly sliced |
| 3 tablespoons fresh chives |
| oil, for shallow frying |
| FOR THE SAUCE |
| 25 g/1 oz green chillies |
| 1 red pepper |
| 200 g/7 oz can tomatoes |
| 1 garlic clove, crushed |
| 1 tablespoon light muscovado sugar |
| 1 tablespoon white wine vinegar |

❶ Make the sauce: seed and chop the chillies and pepper and place with tomatoes and garlic in a pan with the sugar and vinegar. Season and simmer for 10 minutes until reduced by half.

❷ Sift the flour, baking powder and chilli powder. Make a well in the centre and add the eggs and 150 ml/¼ pint water, mixing to make a smooth batter. Stir in the onions, chives and seasoning.

❸ Heat the oil until a bread cube sizzles without burning. Fry spoonfuls of the batter for about 5 minutes on each side until golden; drain on kitchen paper. Serve hot or cold with the sauce.

● *Per serving: calories 400, fat high, saturated fat medium, protein medium, fibre medium, sodium high*

Strawberry and cucumber salad

● **Total time: 25 minutes**
● **Budget** ● **Serves 4**

juice of 1 orange
2 tablespoons roughly chopped fresh mint
freshly ground black pepper
225 g/8 oz strawberries, hulled
1 mini cucumber or ½ small cucumber
fresh mint sprigs, to serve

① Mix together the orange juice, mint and season with freshly ground black pepper. Halve the strawberries, then add to the orange juice mixture, stirring to coat. Cover and set aside for 10–15 minutes to allow the flavours to develop.

② Using a swivel-action peeler or a sharp knife, pare the cucumber into long, thin ribbons. Arrange the ribbons on individual serving plates with the strawberries, pouring over the juice. Season to taste with freshly ground black pepper and chill until ready to serve. Add a sprig of mint to each plate before serving.

● *Per serving: calories 22, fat low, saturated fat low, protein low, fibre high, sodium low*

Falafel with a cucumber dressing

- Total time: 20 minutes
- Budget ● Serves 4–6

400 g/14 oz can chick peas,
drained and rinsed

1 small onion, quartered

1 garlic clove, crushed

½ teaspoon each ground
coriander and cumin

1 egg yolk

50 g/2 oz fresh white
breadcrumbs

olive oil, for frying

FOR THE DRESSING

150 g/5 oz Greek yogurt

a little lemon juice

50 g/2 oz grated cucumber,
squeezed dry

pinch of paprika

1 Make the dressing: mix together the yogurt, lemon juice, cucumber and seasoning. Sprinkle with paprika, and chill.

2 Place the chick peas, onion, garlic, spices, egg yolk and seasoning in a food processor and blend until smooth. Stir in the breadcrumbs.

3 Divide the falafel mixture into 20 pieces, roll into balls and flatten slightly. Heat a little olive oil in a pan and fry the falafel for 2–3 minutes on each side until golden brown. Serve at once with lemon wedges, mixed salad leaves and the dressing.

- *Per serving: calories 251, fat high, saturated fat medium, protein medium, fibre low, sodium high*

Red hot pork ribs

- **Total time: 35 minutes**
- **Average** ● **Serves 4**

1 kg/2 lb lean pork spare ribs
FOR THE MARINADE
2 garlic cloves, crushed
4 tablespoons tomato ketchup or tomato purée
2 tablespoons clear honey
1 tablespoon Dijon mustard
½ teaspoon chilli powder or 1 small fresh chilli, seeded and finely chopped
dash of Worcestershire sauce
seasoning
onion rings, lemon wedges and thyme sprigs, to garnish

① Place the ribs in a shallow, non-metallic dish. Mix together the garlic, tomato ketchup or purée, honey, mustard, chilli, Worcestershire sauce and seasoning. Pour the marinade over the ribs and turn to coat.

② Grill the ribs for 25–30 minutes, turning frequently, until the meat is tender. Serve hot garnished with the onion rings, lemon wedges and thyme sprigs. Provide everyone with a small bowl of warm water and large napkins to wipe their sticky fingers.

● *Per serving: calories 681, fat high, saturated fat high, protein high, fibre medium, sodium medium*

Camembert filo parcels

- **Total time: 30 minutes**
- **Average** ● **Serves 4**

6 sheets filo pastry, thawed if frozen

4 Camembert wedges, about 40 g/1½ oz each

4 teaspoons cranberry sauce

freshly ground black pepper

25 g/1 oz butter, melted

mixed green salad, to serve

① Preheat the oven to 200°C/400°F/Gas 6. Cut the sheets of filo pastry in half to make 12 rectangles. Place three squares on top of each other, rotating each to create a jagged edge.

② Place a wedge of Camembert in the centre of each pastry layer and put a teaspoon of cranberry sauce on top; season with black pepper. Fold over the pastry to enclose the filling, brushing the edges with butter to seal them.

③ Bunch up the ends to make parcels and brush all over with the butter. Bake for about 15 minutes or until golden brown. Leave to cool for 5 minutes before serving with the salad.

● *Per serving: calories 245, fat high, saturated fat high, protein medium, fibre low, sodium low*

Skewered spicy pork

- Total time: 25 minutes
- Cheap ● Serves 4–6

FOR THE MEATBALLS
3 tablespoons ground roasted peanuts

350 g/12 oz minced pork

4 spring onions, finely chopped

1 tablespoon soy sauce

3 tablespoons creamed coconut

1 teaspoon curry powder

½ teaspoon salt

FOR THE TZATZIKI
225 g/8 oz Greek yogurt

1 garlic clove, crushed

½ small cucumber, finely diced

1 teaspoon mint sauce

seasoning

① Mix meatball ingredients together and divide into 24 walnut-sized balls. Flatten to form 1 cm/½ in patties, thread three on to each skewer. Place under a medium hot grill for 6–8 minutes, turning once.

② Mix the tzatziki ingredients together and serve as a sauce.

● *Per serving: calories 430, fat high, saturated fat high, protein high, fibre medium, sodium high*

Herby corn on the cob

- Total time: 20 minutes
- Cheap ● Serves 4

4 heads sweetcorn	3 tablespoons chopped mixed
FOR THE DRESSING	herbs, such as parsley, chives
4 tablespoons olive oil	and coriander
1 tablespoon lemon juice	seasoning
1 garlic clove, crushed	crusty bread, to serve

1 To make the dressing, place the olive oil, lemon juice, garlic, mixed herbs and seasoning in a screw-topped jar. Secure the lid and shake vigorously until it is well combined.

2 Strip the husks and threads off the sweetcorn. Place in a large pan of boiling water, bring back to the boil and cook for 8–10 minutes or until tender. Drain the sweetcorn, drizzle the herb dressing on top and serve with the crusty bread.

● *Per serving: calories 206, fat high, saturated fat medium, protein low, fibre medium, sodium high*

Tuna and runner bean salad

- Total time: 20 minutes
- Cheap • Serves 4

225 g/8 oz runner beans, cut into 4 cm/1½ in diagonal pieces	25 g/1 oz walnut pieces
	FOR THE DRESSING
200 g/7 oz can tuna in brine, drained and flaked	4 tablespoons olive oil
	2 tablespoons white wine vinegar or cider vinegar
2 tomatoes, cut into wedges	1 teaspoon wholegrain mustard
75 g/3 oz button mushrooms, sliced	seasoning

1 Bring a pan of salted water to the boil and blanch the runner beans for 3 minutes. Drain and refresh in cold water, so they retain their bright colour. Place the beans in a serving bowl and mix with the tuna, tomatoes, mushrooms and walnuts.

2 For the dressing, place the olive oil, vinegar, mustard and seasoning in a small bowl and whisk until thoroughly blended. Drizzle over the salad, lightly toss and serve in small bowls.

- *Per serving: calories 343, fat high, saturated fat medium, protein medium, fibre medium, sodium medium*

Roasted pepper salad

- Total time: 40 minutes
- Cheap ● Serves 4

1 red and 2 yellow peppers	2 tablespoons extra virgin olive
3 tomatoes	oil
3 tablespoons freshly grated	seasoning
Parmesan	2 tablespoons chopped fresh
2 garlic cloves, finely chopped	flatleaf parsley, to garnish
12 black olives	crusty bread, to serve

1 Preheat the oven to 200°C/400°F/Gas 6. Cut the peppers in half and remove the seeds, then cut into quarters. Arrange in a lightly oiled, shallow ovenproof dish, cut side up.

2 Drop the tomatoes into a bowl of boiling water, leave for 1 minute and drain. Peel off the skins and cut into quarters. Place one tomato quarter in each piece of pepper and scatter Parmesan and garlic on top. Place a black olive on each piece of pepper and drizzle over the olive oil. Season and roast for 30 minutes until tender.

3 Scatter over the parsley and serve warm or at room temperature with plenty of crusty bread to mop up the juices.

- *Per serving: calories 295, fat medium, saturated fat medium, protein medium, fibre high, sodium high*

Green vegetable risotto

- Total time: 35 minutes
- Budget ● Serves 4

2 tablespoons olive oil	2–3 tablespoons chopped fresh parsley
1 small onion, finely chopped	
225 g/8 oz arborio rice	seasoning
900 ml/1½ pints vegetable or chicken stock	50 g/2 oz Parmesan, finely pared, to garnish
225 g/8 oz mixed green vegetables, such as frozen peas, mangetout, broccoli florets and French beans, trimmed if necessary	

1 Heat the oil in a large, heavy-based pan and fry the onion over a medium heat until it softens and starts to brown.

2 Add to the arborio rice and stir until thoroughly coated in oil. Pour in about 85 ml/3 fl oz of the stock and cook uncovered, stirring occasionally, until the liquid has been absorbed. Add the French beans, if using.

3 Pour in the remaining stock a little at a time. When half has been added, stir in the remaining vegetables and continue cooking and adding stock until the rice is just ready and all of the stock has been absorbed. Stir in the parsley, season to taste and scatter with Parmesan. Leave to rest for 5 minutes before serving.

- *Per serving: calories 351, fat medium, saturated fat medium, protein medium, fibre high, sodium high*

Mixed bean and bacon soup

- **Total time: 30 minutes**
- **Cheap • Serves 4–6**

2 tablespoons olive oil	1 tablespoon chopped fresh
1 onion, thinly sliced	oregano or 1 teaspoon dried
175 g/6 oz smoked bacon, diced	400 g/14 oz can plum tomatoes
2 garlic cloves, chopped	400 g/14 oz can mixed beans
2 carrots, sliced	seasoning
1 celery stick, sliced	warm crusty bread, to serve
900 ml/1½ pints vegetable stock	

1 Heat the oil in a large pan and fry the onion, bacon and half of the garlic for 5 minutes.

2 Add the remaining garlic, carrots, celery, stock, oregano and seasoning. Drain tomatoes and add all of the liquid to the soup. Cover and simmer for 15–20 minutes. Roughly chop the tomatoes and set aside.

3 Drain the beans and add to the pan with the chopped tomatoes. Cover and cook for another 3–4 minutes until heated through. Season to taste and serve hot with crusty bread.

- *Per serving: calories 451, fat medium, saturated fat medium, protein medium, fibre medium, sodium high*

Lamb sauté with basil

● **Total time: 30 minutes**
● **Average ● Serves 4**

25 g/1 oz fresh basil leaves
1 garlic clove, crushed
4 tablespoons olive oil
100 g/4 oz carrots, cut into chunks
100 g/4 oz turnips, cut into chunks
150 g/5 oz fresh or frozen peas
150 g/5 oz French beans, halved
450 g/1 lb lamb fillet, sliced crossways
5 tablespoons lamb stock
seasoning
bread rolls, to serve

❶ Blend the basil, garlic, two tablespoons of the olive oil and plenty of seasoning in a food processor or liquidiser to form a smooth paste. Transfer to a small bowl and set aside.

❷ Heat the remaining oil in a large sauté pan and add the carrots, turnips, peas and beans. Cover and cook over a low heat, shaking the pan occasionally, for 15 minutes or until the vegetables have lightly browned and are just tender.

❸ Push the vegetables to the side of the pan, add the lamb and fry over a high heat for about 5 minutes until browned. Pour in the stock, then gradually stir in the basil paste and cook for 2–3 minutes until you have a smooth sauce. Serve the lamb hot with the bread rolls to mop up the juices.

● *Per serving: calories 425, fat medium, saturated fat high, protein high, fibre high, sodium medium*

Pork with apricots and rosemary

- Total time: 25 minutes
- Cheap ● Serves 4

100 g/4 oz ready-to-eat apricots, finely chopped
1 teaspoon chopped fresh rosemary
4 spring onions, finely chopped
1 garlic clove, crushed
1 tablespoon Dijon mustard
4 boneless loin pork chops, about 100 g/4 oz each
1 tablespoon lemon juice
1 tablespoon clear honey
seasoning
baby new potatoes and sugar snap peas, to serve (optional)

1 Mix together the apricots, rosemary, spring onions, garlic, Dijon mustard and seasoning in a small bowl.

2 Make a slit in the side of each pork chop and carefully continue to cut through to make a pocket. Fill with the apricot mixture.

3 Mix lemon juice and honey and brush over the chops. Grill for about 7 minutes on each side until tender and cooked through. Serve at once with new potatoes and sugar snap peas.

● *Per serving: calories 372, fat medium, saturated fat medium, protein high, fibre high, sodium low*

Ham rösti

- Total time: 25 minutes
- Budget • Serves 4

1 kg/2 lb waxy potatoes, such as Charlotte or Désirée, cooked in skins
175 g/6 oz cooked ham, cubed
4 tablespoons chopped fresh parsley, plus extra to garnish
50 g/2 oz Cheddar, grated
25 g/1 oz butter
2 tablespoons vegetable oil
seasoning
fresh parsley, to garnish
grilled tomatoes and baby sweetcorn, to serve

1 Peel and coarsely grate the potatoes. Place in a bowl, season well and mix in the ham, parsley and Cheddar. Heat half of the butter and oil in a 25 cm/10 in heavy-based frying pan and add the potato mixture, pressing it down evenly. Cook for 10 minutes or until the base is golden and crispy.

2 Invert the rösti onto a plate. Heat the remaining butter and oil and slide the rösti back into the pan, uncooked side down; cook for another 10 minutes. Slide out on to a warmed plate and garnish with parsley. Cut into wedges and serve hot with the grilled tomatoes and baby sweetcorn.

- *Per serving: calories 456, fat medium, saturated fat high, protein medium, fibre high, sodium high*

Curried lamb with potatoes

- Total time: 30 minutes
- Cheap • Serves 4

225 g/8 oz baby new potatoes, scrubbed and halved
2 tablespoons vegetable oil
1 onion, finely chopped
1 garlic clove, crushed
450 g/1 lb neck fillet of lamb, cubed
1 tablespoon mild curry powder
400 g/14 oz can chopped tomatoes
½ lamb stock cube, crumbled
225 g/8 oz baby sweetcorn
seasoning
fresh coriander, to garnish
rice, poppodums and a yogurt *raita*, to serve

1 Parboil the potatoes in a pan of boiling salted water for 10 minutes; drain. Heat the oil in a large pan and fry the onion and garlic until lightly browned.

2 Stir in the lamb and cook, stirring, for about 5 minutes. Add the curry powder, chopped tomatoes and stock cube and cook gently for 10–15 minutes.

3 Add the potatoes and baby sweetcorn, season to taste and cook for about 5 minutes. Garnish with the herbs. Serve at once with rice, poppodums and a yogurt *raita*.

- *Per serving: calories 652, fat medium, saturated fat medium, protein high, fibre medium, sodium high*

Chilli bean and sausage casserole

- Total time: 35 minutes
- Cheap ● Serves 4

2 tablespoons olive oil
1 large onion, chopped
225 g/8 oz cocktail sausages
2 garlic cloves, crushed
2 teaspoons chilli powder
good pinch of cayenne pepper
(optional)
2 x 400 g/14 oz cans chopped
tomatoes
1 tablespoon tomato purée
dash of Worcestershire sauce
2 small courgettes, sliced
100 g/4 oz sweetcorn
400 g/14 oz can red kidney
beans, drained and rinsed
seasoning

1 Heat the oil and fry the onion and sausages for 10 minutes until the onions have softened and the sausages are browned. Stir in garlic, chilli powder and cayenne pepper (if using) and cook, stirring, for 30 seconds.

2 Stir in the tomatoes, tomato purée, Worcestershire sauce and seasoning and bring to the boil. Simmer for 15 minutes.

3 Add courgettes, sweetcorn and kidney beans, cover and simmer for 5 minutes. Serve with soured cream and tortilla chips and garnish with parsley.

● *Per serving: calories 658, fat high, saturated fat high, protein medium, fibre high, sodium high*

Tangy lamb burgers

● **Total time: 25 minutes**
● **Budget** ● **Serves 4**

2 tablespoons tomato ketchup
1 teaspoon Dijon mustard
dash of Worcestershire sauce
450 g/1 lb lean minced lamb
1 small onion, chopped
2 pitta breads
few lettuce leaves
seasoning
tomato and onion salad, to serve

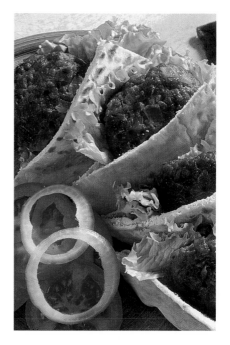

❶ Mix together the tomato ketchup, mustard and Worcestershire sauce in a bowl. Add the lamb, onion and seasoning and mix well. With dampened hands, shape the mixture into eight small burgers or four large ones, if you prefer.

❷ Grill the burgers for about 4 minutes on each side until golden brown and cooked through. Toast the pitta breads, cut each one into two or four and place a burger and some lettuce in each one. Serve hot with the tomato and onion salad.

● *Per serving: calories 413, fat high, saturated fat high, protein high, fibre medium, sodium medium*

Pastrami and new potato salad

- Total time: 25 minutes
- Cheap ● Serves 4

---

175 g/6 oz small new potatoes

---

3 tablespoons olive oil

---

2 teaspoons white wine vinegar

---

1 tablespoon wholegrain mustard

---

1 teaspoon sugar

---

200 g/7 oz bag mixed salad leaves

---

100 g/4 oz pastrami, cut into small strips

---

50 g/2 oz button mushrooms, sliced

---

50 g/2 oz radishes, sliced

---

seasoning

---

❶ Cook the potatoes in boiling, salted water for 15–20 minutes until they are tender.

❷ Meanwhile, make the dressing: place the oil, vinegar, mustard, sugar and seasoning in a screw-topped jar and shake well to mix.

❸ Drain the potatoes, halve or slice them, then toss in half of the dressing. Arrange the salad leaves in a bowl and top with the potatoes, pastrami, mushrooms and radishes. Drizzle over the remaining dressing and serve at once.

- *Per serving: calories 175, fat high, saturated fat medium, protein medium, fibre low, sodium medium*

Spaghetti with smoked bacon and mushrooms

- Total time: 20 minutes
- Cheap ● Serves 4

350 g/12 oz fresh or dried
spaghetti

4 tablespoons olive oil

2 garlic cloves, finely chopped

225 g/8 oz smoked streaky
bacon, chopped

100 g/4 oz button mushrooms,
sliced

400 g/14 oz tomatoes, seeded
and roughly chopped

4 tablespoons chopped fresh
herbs, such as basil, marjoram
or parsley

seasoning

fresh herbs and Parmesan
shavings, to garnish

❶ Cook the pasta in a large pan of boiling salted water until *al dente*. Drain and toss with two tablespoons of the olive oil. Transfer to a serving dish, cover and keep warm.

❷ Heat the remaining oil in a frying pan and fry the garlic and bacon until golden. Add the mushrooms and continue cooking for 2–3 minutes.

❸ Stir in the tomatoes, herbs and seasoning and cook for 2–3 minutes until hot. Tip the sauce onto the pasta; leave covered for 1 minute. Toss again and serve at once, garnished with the herbs and Parmesan.

- *Per serving: calories 744, fat high, saturated fat medium, protein medium, fibre medium, sodium high*

Moroccan lamb koftas

- **Total time: 30 minutes**
- **Cheap ● Serves 4**

450 g/1 lb minced lamb
2 garlic cloves, crushed
1 teaspoon ground cumin
4 tablespoons chopped fresh mint
50 g/2 oz ready-to-eat apricots, chopped
1 tablespoon olive oil
1–2 tablespoons mango chutney
2 teaspoons cornflour, blended with a little water
150 g/5 oz carton natural yogurt
seasoning
rice and a green salad, to serve

1 Combine the lamb, garlic, cumin, half of the mint and the apricots; shape into 24 small balls.

2 Fry the meatballs in the oil until cooked through and golden. Remove from the pan with a slotted spoon and drain off any excess fat.

3 Add the chutney and 50 ml/2 fl oz of water to pan. Bring to boil, scraping sediment from bottom. Return meatballs to the pan; heat through.

4 Blend cornflour mixture with yogurt; add to the pan gradually and cook gently until it is thickened; do not boil. Garnish with remaining mint and serve with rice and a green salad.

- *Per serving: calories 277, fat medium, saturated fat high, protein high, fibre low, sodium medium*

Liver with sage and apple

- Total time: 25 minutes
- Average ● Serves 4

450 g/1 lb lambs' liver, cut
into strips

a little seasoned plain flour

2 tablespoons olive oil

1 onion, cut into rings

2 small, red-skinned apples,
cored, seeded and cut into
wedges

few sage leaves, bruised

300 ml/½ pint unsweetened
apple juice

2 tablespoons tomato purée

2 teaspoons Dijon mustard

4 tablespoons fromage frais

seasoning

1 Coat the liver strips on both sides in the seasoned flour. Heat the oil in a deep frying pan and gently fry the onion for about 5 minutes until softened.

2 Push the onions aside, then add the liver and fry for 2–3 minutes on each side. Add the apples and sage leaves to the pan and fry for another 5 minutes, stirring occasionally. Stir in the apple juice and tomato purée, bring to the boil and simmer for about 5 minutes.

3 Stir in the mustard, fromage frais and seasoning and simmer gently for 1–2 minutes. Serve at once with mashed potato and sprouting broccoli.

- *Per serving: calories 437, fat medium, saturated fat medium, protein high, fibre low, sodium medium*

Leek and bacon tortilla

- Total time: 25 minutes
- Budget ● Serves 4

1 tablespoon sunflower oil
2 leeks, chopped
225 g/8 oz frozen mixed vegetables e.g. broccoli, cauliflower and carrots
100 g/4 oz cooked ham, chopped
3 eggs
100 g/4 oz curd cheese
150 ml/¼ pint milk
2 tablespoons dried white breadcrumbs
seasoning
mixed salad, to serve

① Heat the oil in a frying pan and fry the leeks for 5 minutes until just cooked through. Cook the vegetables in a separate pan of boiling salted water for about 5 minutes until tender. Drain.

② Remove the frying pan from the heat and scatter over the vegetables and ham.

③ Beat the eggs, cheese and seasoning until frothy, add the milk and beat again. Pour into frying pan and sprinkle breadcrumbs on top.

④ Return the pan to the heat and cook gently for about 5 minutes until the tortilla is beginning to set.

⑤ Grill for another 5 minutes until cooked through and bubbling. Serve warm, cut into wedges, with the salad.

- *Per serving: calories 211, fat high, saturated fat high, protein high, fibre medium, sodium high*

Smoked sausage cassoulet

- Total time: 30 minutes
- Cheap ● Serves 4

2 tablespoons olive oil
12 small onions
1 garlic clove, crushed
350 g/12 oz smoked sausage, such as chorizo, cut into chunks
400 g/14 oz can butter beans, drained
400 g/14 oz can flageolet beans, drained
400 g/14 oz can chopped tomatoes with herbs
1 tablespoon tomato purée
1 tablespoon Dijon mustard
seasoning
2 tablespoons chopped fresh parsley, to garnish

1 Heat the oil in a large pan and fry the onions and garlic for 5 minutes until soft. Add the smoked sausage pieces, butter beans, flageolet beans, chopped tomatoes, tomato purée, Dijon mustard and seasoning to the pan and mix together well.

2 Bring the mixture to the boil, then reduce the heat, cover and cook for about 20 minutes until heated through.

3 Sprinkle with the parsley and serve immediately, with new potatoes if you wish.

- *Per serving: calories 774, fat medium, saturated fat high, protein medium, fibre medium, sodium high*

Spicy couscous with lamb

- Total time: 30 minutes
- Average ● Serves 4

2 tablespoons olive oil	
1 onion, finely chopped	
225 g/8 oz couscous	
450 ml/¾ pint chicken or vegetable stock	
2 tablespoons mild curry paste	
2 tablespoons tomato or mango chutney	
2 teaspoons ground paprika	
50 g/2 oz raisins	
8 loin lamb chops	
2–3 tablespoons chopped fresh coriander	
7.5 cm/3 in piece cucumber, seeded and diced	
1 red apple, diced	

1 Heat the oil and fry the onion until softened. Add couscous and cook gently for 2 minutes. In another pan, mix the stock, curry paste, chutney, paprika and raisins; bring to the boil.

2 Add the curry mixture to the couscous, mix well and remove from the heat. Cover tightly and leave for 20 minutes.

3 Meanwhile, grill the lamb chops for 6–8 minutes on each side. Uncover the couscous, and stir in the coriander, cucumber and apple. Season, then serve with the lamb and poppodums.

● *Per serving: calories 668, fat medium, saturated fat high, protein high, fibre low, sodium medium*

Bean and bacon feast

- Total time: 25 minutes
- Budget ● Serves 4

1 tablespoon olive oil
1 onion, chopped
3 carrots, diced
2 large potatoes, diced
175 g/6 oz smoked bacon, chopped
400 g/14 oz can baked beans
1 teaspoon Worcestershire sauce
2 slices wholemeal bread, crusts removed
1 teaspoon fresh thyme leaves
25 g/1 oz Cheddar, grated
seasoning

❶ Heat the oil and fry the onion, carrots and potatoes for about 10 minutes, stirring until just cooked through and lightly golden. Add the bacon and cook for 2–3 minutes.

❷ Add beans, Worcestershire sauce and seasoning and heat through. Place the bread and thyme in a food processor and whizz until it forms crumbs. Add Cheddar.

❸ Tip the bean mixture into an ovenproof dish, sprinkle over the breadcrumb mixture and grill until toasted and bubbling. Serve hot.

- *Per serving: calories 303, fat medium, saturated fat medium, protein high, fibre high, sodium high*

Mini meatball pitta pockets

- Total time: 20 minutes
- Average ● Serves 4

275 g/10 oz minced lamb
1 garlic clove, crushed
2 tablespoons chopped fresh mint or parsley
½ teaspoon ground cinnamon
1 egg yolk, beaten
4 pitta bread
3 carrots, cut into slivers
10 cm/4 in piece cucumber, halved and sliced
4 tomatoes, seeded and diced
4 tablespoons natural yogurt
1 teaspoon snipped fresh chives
seasoning
mixed green salad, to serve

1 Mix the lamb with the garlic, mint or parsley, cinnamon, egg yolk and seasoning. Shape into 24 small balls and grill, turning once, for 5 minutes until cooked through. Transfer to a plate and keep warm until required.

2 Grill the pitta for about 30 seconds on each side, then cut in half and gently ease open each one to make a pocket. Fill each pitta pocket with four meatballs and add some carrot, cucumber and tomato.

3 Mix the yogurt and chives and drizzle over the pitta filling. Serve with a mixed green salad.

- *Per serving: calories 578, fat medium, saturated fat high, protein medium, fibre medium, sodium medium*

Lamb with lentils

- **Total time: 30 minutes**
- **Average ● Serves 4**

2 tablespoons olive oil	300 ml/½ pint lamb stock
450 g/1 lb leg of lamb, cut into chunks	4 tomatoes, peeled and cut into wedges
1 onion, roughly chopped	1 tablespoon chopped fresh parsley
2 garlic cloves, crushed	
1 teaspoon ground coriander	seasoning
1 teaspoon ground cumin	plain boiled rice and naan bread, to serve
100 g/4 oz red lentils	
1 tablespoon tomato purée	

1 Heat the olive oil in a large pan, then add the lamb and fry for about 5 minutes until browned all over. Add the onion, garlic, coriander, cumin and seasoning and continue to cook for a further 3–4 minutes, stirring occasionally.

2 Add the lentils and tomato purée to the pan, then pour in the lamb stock and bring to the boil. Reduce the heat, cover and simmer for about 20 minutes until the lentils are cooked and most of the stock is absorbed.

3 Stir in the tomatoes and parsley and heat through. Serve hot with plain boiled rice and naan bread.

- *Per serving: calories 614, fat medium, saturated fat high, protein medium, fibre low, sodium medium*

Honey-glazed sausages

- **Total time: 35 minutes**
- **Budget** ● **Serves 4**

4 baking potatoes, cut in half lengthways	**2 tablespoons soy sauce**
	2 tablespoons clear honey
450 g/1 lb thick pork sausages	**seasoning**
2 teaspoons wholegrain mustard	**baked beans, to serve**

1 Preheat the oven to 200°C/400°F/Gas 6. Place the potatoes with the skin side up on a wire rack set on a baking sheet. Bake for 30–35 minutes until the flesh is tender when pierced with a skewer.

2 Lightly prick the sausages with a fork. Mix together the mustard, soy sauce, honey and seasoning and brush over the sausages, then arrange them in an ovenproof dish and add 3 tablespoons water to prevent the glaze from sticking to the dish.

3 Bake the sausages for 25 minutes, basting and turning occasionally. Serve with the potatoes and baked beans.

- *Per serving: calories 756, fat medium, saturated fat high, protein medium, fibre high, sodium high*

Speedy shepherd's pie

● **Total time: 30 minutes**
● **Budget** ● **Serves 4**

450 g/1 lb potatoes, cut into chunks	**2 tablespoons tomato purée**
450 g/1 lb swede, cut into small chunks	**1 tablespoon Worcestershire sauce**
knob of butter	**1 teaspoon chopped fresh rosemary or ½ teaspoon dried**
450 g/1 lb lean minced lamb	**seasoning**
1 large onion, chopped	**steamed broccoli florets, to serve**
1 teaspoon plain flour	
1 lamb stock cube	

❶ Cook potatoes and swede in a pan of boiling salted water for 15–20 minutes. Drain, return to the pan and mash with plenty of black pepper and the butter.

❷ Meanwhile, heat a frying pan and dry fry the lamb with the onion, stirring until the onion is softened and the lamb browned. Remove from heat; stir in flour.

❸ Dissolve stock cube in 300 ml/½ pint boiling water, then add to the pan with the tomato purée, Worcestershire sauce, rosemary and seasoning. Return the pan to the heat and simmer for 10–15 minutes until sauce has thickened and lamb is tender.

❹ Tip the lamb mixture into a heatproof casserole and spread over the mashed potato and swede, swirling with the back of a spoon. Grill until bubbling and golden; serve with the broccoli.

● *Per serving: calories 427, fat medium, saturated fat high, protein high, fibre medium, sodium medium*

Bacon chops with root vegetable rösti

- Total time: 30 minutes
- Cheap • Serves 4

300 g/11 oz potatoes, grated	2 tablespoons olive oil
225 g/8 oz carrots, grated	4 thick-cut bacon chops
100 g/4 oz swede, grated	2 tomatoes, halved
100 g/4 oz parsnips, grated	seasoning
100 g/4 oz turnips, grated	Dijon mustard, to serve
4 tablespoons snipped fresh chives	flatleaf parsley, to garnish
2 tablespoons chopped fresh parsley	

❶ Preheat the grill. Squeeze out the excess liquid and starch from the potatoes, carrots, swede, parsnips and turnips. Place them in a large bowl and mix together well. Stir in half of the chives, half of the parsley and add the seasoning.

❷ Heat the oil in a pan and fry heaped tablespoonfuls of the vegetable mixture for about 5 minutes on each side until crisp and golden.

❸ Meanwhile, grill the chops for 4–5 minutes, turn them over, placing the tomatoes under the grill at the same time, and cook for 3–4 minutes. Spoon over a little mustard, sprinkle with the remaining herbs and garnish with the flatleaf parsley.

- *Per serving: calories 295, fat medium, saturated fat medium, protein high, fibre high, sodium high*

One-pot spicy lamb

- Total time: 40 minutes
- Average ● Serves 4

4 best end of neck lamb chops	2 small parsnips, thickly sliced
2 tablespoons olive oil	4 carrots, thickly sliced
2 tablespoons plain flour	6 potatoes, peeled and
2 teaspoons ground cumin	quartered
1 teaspoon ground coriander	1 tablespoon chopped fresh
600 ml/1 pint lamb stock	rosemary
2 tablespoons tomato purée	seasoning
1 small swede, roughly chopped	

1 Fry the chops in the oil for 2–3 minutes on each side. Remove the lamb from the pan and set aside. Add the flour, cumin and coriander to the pan and cook, stirring, for 2–3 minutes.

2 Mix together the stock and tomato purée and whisk in a little at a time. Return the chops to the pan and add the swede, parsnips, carrots, potatoes, rosemary and seasoning. Bring to the boil, cover and simmer for about 20 minutes until all of the vegetables are tender.

● *Per serving: calories 807, fat high, saturated fat high, protein medium, fibre medium, sodium medium*

Quick beef stroganoff

- **Total time: 25 minutes**
- **Average • Serves 4**

450 g/1 lb rump steak, cut into strips	**1 tablespoon tomato purée**
a little ground paprika	**150 ml/¼ pint soured cream**
25 g/1 oz butter	**dash of lemon juice**
1 tablespoon vegetable oil	**seasoning**
150 g/5 oz mushrooms, sliced	**chopped fresh coriander, to garnish**
4 spring onions, trimmed and chopped	**boiled rice and soured cream, to serve**

1 Sprinkle the steak with paprika and seasoning. Heat the butter and oil in a pan, add the steak and fry on both sides for about 5 minutes until it is well browned.

2 Add the mushrooms and spring onions, then stir in the tomato purée and soured cream and simmer for a few minutes. Add a dash of lemon juice and seasoning and garnish with the coriander. Serve hot with boiled rice and a dollop of soured cream on top, if you wish.

- *Per serving: calories 587, fat medium, saturated fat high, protein high, fibre low, sodium medium*

Baked aromatic chicken

- Total time: 40 minutes
- Budget ● Serves 4

2 tablespoons clear honey

1 tablespoon wholegrain mustard

2 teaspoons medium hot curry powder

8 chicken thighs, skinned

150 g/5 oz natural low-fat yogurt

25 g/1 oz flaked almonds, toasted

plain boiled rice, chutney and naan bread, to serve

1 Preheat the oven to 200°C/400°F/Gas 6. Mix together the honey, mustard and curry powder until combined. Place chicken thighs in a roasting tin and brush with the sauce until well coated.

2 Pour 120 ml/4 fl oz water into the tin and bake uncovered for 25–30 minutes until the chicken is cooked through and nicely browned.

3 Transfer the chicken to a serving dish and keep warm. Place the roasting tin on the hob and bring the pan juices to the boil, then simmer until reduced by half. Stir in the yogurt, a spoonful at a time, over a low heat so it doesn't curdle. Pour the sauce over the chicken. Scatter over the flaked almonds and serve with the boiled rice, chutney and naan bread.

- *Per serving: calories 664, fat medium, saturated fat low, protein high, fibre low, sodium medium*

Fried noodles with chicken livers

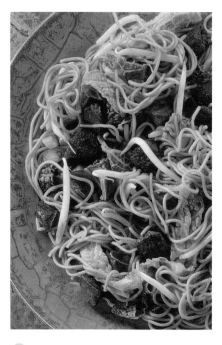

● **Total time: 30 minutes**
● **Budget** ● **Serves 4**

225 g/8 oz chicken livers, thawed if frozen, chopped
5 tablespoons soy sauce
200 g/7 oz thread egg noodles
3 tablespoons vegetable oil
4 garlic cloves, crushed
2.5 cm/1 in piece fresh root ginger, finely chopped
175 g/6 oz cabbage or spring greens, shredded
175 g/6 oz beansprouts
4 spring onions, chopped

1 Place the chicken livers with the soy sauce in a bowl and mix well; leave to marinate for 15 minutes.

2 Place the noodles in a pan of boiling water, remove from the heat and set aside for 4 minutes, then drain and toss in half of the oil.

3 Heat the remaining oil in a wok or frying pan. Using a slotted spoon, add the livers (reserving soy sauce) with the garlic and ginger and stir-fry for 2 minutes.

4 Add the cabbage or spring greens and beansprouts and stir-fry for 1–2 minutes, then tip in the noodles and stir fry for 2–3 minutes. Pour in the reserved soy sauce and spring onions; stir-fry for 1 minute. Serve at once.

● *Per serving: calories 418, fat medium, saturated fat low, protein medium, fibre medium, sodium low*

Braised stuffed chicken

- ● Total time: 30 minutes
- ● Average ● Serves 4

25 g/1 oz butter
2 tablespoons freshly grated Parmesan
2 teaspoons chopped fresh rosemary
4 chicken breasts, about 150 g/5 oz each, boned
1 tablespoon vegetable oil
300 ml/½ pint chicken stock
1 tablespoon tomato purée
4 carrots, sliced
2 parsnips, cut into chunks
1 potato, diced
2 leeks, sliced
seasoning
4 parsley sprigs, to garnish

1 Mash together the butter, Parmesan, rosemary and seasoning. Lift the skin on each chicken breast and spread the butter mixture underneath, then smooth the skin back over the chicken fillets.

2 Heat the oil in a large pan and fry the chicken for 2–3 minutes on each side until lightly browned. Remove from the pan and set aside. Stir in the stock, tomato purée, carrot, parsnip, potato and leeks.

3 Arrange the chicken on top of the vegetables, bring to the boil, then cover and cook for 20–30 minutes until tender. Garnish and serve with boiled brown rice.

● *Per serving: calories 592, fat medium, saturated fat medium, protein high, fibre medium, sodium medium*

Spicy chicken kebabs

- Total time: 30 minutes
- Average ● Serves 4

50 g/2 oz unsalted cashew nuts
10 skinless chicken thighs, boned and cubed
225 g/8 oz Greek strained yogurt
25 g/1 oz piece fresh root ginger, peeled and crushed
4 garlic cloves, crushed
juice of 1 lemon
1 teaspoon ground cumin
good pinch of cayenne pepper
seasoning
mango chutney, lime wedges and mixed rice, to serve

① Spread the cashew nuts on a sheet of aluminium foil, then place under the grill and lightly toast. When the cashews are cool, place in a polythene bag and crush to a fine paste with a rolling pin.

② Place the chicken in a shallow, non-metallic dish. Mix together the yogurt, ginger, garlic, cashew nuts, lemon juice, cumin, cayenne and seasoning to taste. Pour over the chicken and turn to coat. Cover and leave to marinate for at least 15 minutes or up to 6 hours.

③ Meanwhile, soak 12 bamboo skewers in cold water for 10–15 minutes. Pat dry, then thread the chicken pieces on to skewers and grill for about 8–10 minutes, turning once. Serve at once with the chutney, lime wedges and mixed rice.

● *Per serving: calories 374, fat medium, saturated fat medium, protein high, fibre low, sodium medium*

Honeyed chicken with rice

- Total time: 35 minutes
- Cheap ● Serves 4

3 tablespoons clear honey

2 tablespoons soy sauce

2 tablespoons orange juice

1 tablespoon wholegrain
mustard

1 garlic clove, crushed

8 chicken drumsticks

1 tablespoon sunflower oil

350 g/12 oz long grain rice

1 chicken stock cube

100 g/4 oz sweetcorn

2 spring onions, chopped

seasoning

flatleaf parsley, to garnish

runner beans and spring onions,
to serve

1 Preheat the oven to 200°C/400°F/Gas 6. Mix together the honey, soy sauce, orange juice, mustard and garlic in an ovenproof dish. Add drumsticks and toss to coat. Bake for 30 minutes, brushing occasionally with the honey mixture.

2 Heat the oil and stir in the rice. Pour over 600 ml/1 pint water, crumble in the stock cube and season. Bring to the boil, cover and cook for 10 minutes. Add the sweetcorn and cook for a further 5 minutes.

3 When the rice is tender, add the chopped onions and fork through the rice. Garnish with parsley and serve with the drumsticks and vegetables.

- *Per serving: calories 561, fat medium, saturated fat low, protein high, fibre low, sodium medium*

Spanish chicken with rice

- Total time: 40 minutes
- Average • Serves 6

450 g/1 lb boneless chicken thighs
½ teaspoon ground paprika
2 tablespoons olive oil
1 large onion, chopped
2 garlic cloves, crushed
225 g/8 oz long grain rice
good pinch of ground turmeric
750 ml/1¼ pints chicken or vegetable stock
225 g/8 oz chorizo sausage, sliced
100 g/4 oz fresh or frozen peas
seasoning
1–2 tablespoons chopped fresh coriander, to garnish

1 Season the chicken and toss in the paprika. Heat the oil and gently fry the chicken, onion and garlic for 5 minutes until golden.

2 Stir in the rice and turmeric and fry gently for 5 minutes, stirring, until the oil is absorbed and the rice becomes opaque.

3 Gradually pour in the stock and cook gently for about 20 minutes, stirring occasionally, until the rice is almost tender.

4 Add the chorizo and peas. Increase the heat and cook for 10 minutes until all the liquid has been absorbed and the chicken is tender. Season generously and garnish with coriander.

- *Per serving: calories 485, fat medium, saturated fat medium, protein high, fibre low, sodium low*

Turkey burgers

- Total time: 35 minutes
- Budget ● Serves 4

450 g/1 lb potatoes, cut into wedges
2 tablespoons olive oil
1 teaspoon coarse sea salt
1 small onion, finely chopped
350 g/12 oz minced turkey
50 g/2 oz fresh white breadcrumbs
grated rind of ½ lemon
3 tablespoons chopped fresh parsley
8 smoked streaky bacon rashers
seasoning

① Preheat the oven to 200°C/400°F/Gas 6. Place the potatoes in an ovenproof dish, drizzle over half of the oil and toss to coat. Sprinkle with the salt and bake for 30–35 minutes until golden.

② Heat the remaining oil and fry the onion until softened. Remove from the heat and mix in the turkey, breadcrumbs, lemon rind, parsley and seasoning.

③ Dust your hands with flour and shape the mixture into four burgers. Wrap two bacon rashers around each one and grill for about 5 minutes on each side. Garnish with parsley sprigs and serve each on a lettuce leaf with the potatoes, carrot and cucumber batons and halved cherry tomatoes.

- *Per serving: calories 526, fat high, saturated fat high, protein high, fibre medium, sodium high*

Quick chicken paella

- Total time: 40 minutes
- Average ● Serves 4

1 tablespoon olive oil
1 onion, chopped
2 garlic cloves, crushed
50 g/2 oz bacon, chopped
8 skinned and boned chicken thighs (about 450 g/1 lb)
100 g/4 oz runner beans, sliced diagonally
300 g/11 oz arborio or risotto rice
200 g/7 oz can chopped tomatoes
pinch of saffron strands, soaked in hot water for 10 minutes
750 ml/1¼ pints chicken stock

① Heat the olive oil in a large, heavy-based pan and gently fry the onion, garlic and bacon for about 5 minutes until just beginning to brown. Season the chicken, add to the pan and cook until lightly browned on all sides. Tip in the beans and stir-fry for 1–2 minutes.

② Add the rice and stir until evenly coated. Add tomatoes, saffron and half of the stock, cover and cook for 10–15 minutes until all of the stock has been absorbed. Pour in the rest of the stock, cover and cook for a further 10 minutes. Season to taste and serve.

- *Per serving: calories 489, fat medium, saturated fat low, protein high, fibre medium, sodium medium*

Speedy coq au vin

- ● Total time: 25 minutes
- ● Average ● Serves 4

2 tablespoons olive oil	150 ml/¼ pint dry red wine
450 g/1 lb boned and skinned chicken, sliced	2 teaspoons Worcestershire sauce
175 g/6 oz button onions, halved	1 tablespoon chopped fresh thyme and a few sprigs, to garnish
175 g/6 oz button mushrooms	
100 g/4 oz lean bacon, diced	mashed potato and mangetout, to serve
450 ml/¾ pint chicken stock	

1 Heat the oil in a sauté pan, add the chicken and cook for 3–4 minutes, stirring occasionally, until it is just beginning to brown. Add the onions, mushrooms and bacon; cook for 3–4 minutes.

2 Pour in the stock, wine and Worcestershire sauce, then add the chopped thyme. Bring to the boil and simmer gently for about 15 minutes. Garnish with thyme sprigs and serve with mashed potato and mangetout.

● *Per serving: calories 458, fat medium, saturated fat medium, protein high, fibre medium, sodium medium*

Paprika chicken

- Total time: 30 minutes
- Average ● Serves 4

3 tablespoons olive oil	good pinch of ground cayenne pepper (optional)
1 onion, sliced	
1 garlic clove, crushed	400 g/14 oz can chopped tomatoes with herbs
8 chicken thighs, skinned	
2 tablespoons plain flour	150 ml/¼ pint chicken or vegetable stock
2 teaspoons ground paprika	
1 red, 1 yellow and 1 green pepper, seeded and cut into strips	seasoning
	flatleaf parsley, to garnish
	boiled potatoes, lightly tossed in parsley butter, to serve
1 bay leaf	

1 Heat the oil in a large frying pan and cook the onion and garlic over a gentle heat until softened. Generously season the chicken and coat in the combined flour and paprika. Add the chicken to the onion and fry for 1–2 minutes on each side until lightly browned.

2 Stir in the peppers, bay leaf and cayenne pepper, if using, and cook, stirring continuously, for 2–3 minutes. Add the tomatoes and stock, bring to the boil and simmer for about 10 minutes until peppers are soft. Season to taste and garnish with flatleaf parsley. Serve with potatoes.

● *Per serving: calories 422, fat medium, saturated fat medium, protein high, fibre medium, sodium high*

Seafood and leek parcels

- Total time: 30 minutes
- Average ● Serves 4

4 leeks, thinly slice

4 x 100 g/4 oz cod fillets,
skinned and boned

100 g/4 oz peeled prawns,
thawed if frozen

2 tablespoons roughly
chopped fresh dill

juice of 1 lemon

25 g/1 oz butter

seasoning

lemon wedges and dill sprigs,
to garnish

① Preheat the oven to 200°C/400°F/Gas 6. Cut out four circles of non-stick baking paper, about 30 cm/12 in diameter. Make a fold in each piece of paper, scatter the leeks over half and place the cod on top.

② Divide the prawns equally among the four parcels, then sprinkle over the chopped dill and season well. Melt the butter in the lemon juice in a small pan, then pour it over the fish.

③ Fold over the clean half of each parcel and roll the edges tightly together. Place on a baking sheet and bake for 10–15 minutes until cooked.

④ Place each parcel on a dinner plate and garnish with a lemon wedge and dill sprig. Serve at once, opening them at the table.

- *Per serving: calories 264, fat medium, saturated fat medium, protein medium, fibre high, sodium high*

Cod steaks with capers

● **Total time: 20 minutes**
● **Average** ● **Serves 4**

2 tablespoons olive oil
100 g/4 oz streaky bacon, rinded and cut into strips
4 cod steaks, about 175 g/6 oz each
50 g/2 oz each fresh parsley and basil, roughly chopped
2 tablespoons capers, drained and chopped
juice of 1 lemon
seasoning
new potatoes and French beans, to serve

1 Heat the oil in a large frying pan and fry the bacon for 3–4 minutes until just crisp. Using a slotted spoon, remove the bacon from the pan and keep warm.

2 Season the cod steaks on both sides. Add to the pan and fry for about 5 minutes on each side until just flaking.

3 Return the bacon to the pan. Add the parsley, basil, capers and lemon juice and cook for a further 2–3 minutes, stirring occasionally. Serve immediately with new potatoes and French beans.

● *Per serving: calories 600, fat high, saturated fat medium, protein high, fibre medium, sodium high*

Salmon fish cakes

- Total time: 30 minutes
- Cheap ● Serves 4

225 g/8 oz potatoes, cut into chunks

1 tablespoon mayonnaise

3 eggs

200 g/7 oz can red salmon, drained

3 tablespoons chopped fresh parsley

2 teaspoons lemon juice

50 g/2 oz fresh white breadcrumbs

vegetable oil, for frying

seasoning

sliced tomato and cucumber, mixed salad leaves, and Greek strained yogurt, to serve

❶ Cook the potatoes in boiling water for about 15 minutes until tender. Drain and mash with the mayonnaise. Boil two of the eggs for 7 minutes, drain, then peel and finely chop.

❷ Place the salmon in a large bowl and add the potato, chopped egg, parsley and lemon juice. Season and mix well. Chill until ready to use.

❸ Dust your hands with flour and shape the salmon mixture into four rounds. Lightly beat the remaining egg, dip the fish cakes in it, then coat in the breadcrumbs.

❹ Fry the fish cakes for about 5 minutes on each side until golden brown. Drain on kitchen paper and serve at once with tomato and cucumber slices, mixed salad leaves and Greek strained yogurt with chopped flatleaf parsley.

- *Per serving: calories 557, fat high, saturated fat low, protein medium, fibre medium, sodium medium*

Spiced smoked haddock pilaff

- Total time: 40 minutes
- Average ● Serves 4

2 eggs
2 tablespoons vegetable oil
1 onion, thinly sliced
2 garlic cloves, crushed
2 teaspoons curry powder
50 g/2 oz flaked almonds
225 g/8 oz brown long grain rice
450 g/1 lb skinless smoked haddock, cubed
175 g/6 oz frozen peas
50 g/2 oz sultanas
seasoning
2 tablespoons chopped fresh parsley, to garnish

❶ Place the eggs in a pan of boiling water, bring back to boil and simmer for 10–12 minutes. Cool under running water, then tap shells. When cold, crack the shells, then peel and chop eggs.

❷ Meanwhile, heat the oil in a heavy-based pan. Add onion and garlic and fry gently for 2–3 minutes. Stir in curry powder and almonds and fry for 2 minutes.

❸ Add rice, stir until coated, then slowly pour in 750 ml/1¼ pints boiling water and bring back to the boil. Stir once and reduce heat to a simmer. Cover and cook gently for 20 minutes.

❹ Remove the lid and scatter the haddock and peas over the rice. Cover and cook for 15 minutes. Add sultanas and fork through gently, season to taste and sprinkle over the egg. Garnish with parsley.

● *Per serving: calories 580, fat medium, saturated fat low, protein high, fibre medium, sodium high*

Steamed trout fillets

- Total time: 30 minutes
- Budget ● Serves 4

4 rainbow trout fillets, about
100–175 g/4–6 oz each

3 slices fresh root ginger,
peeled and finely shredded

2 tablespoons light soy sauce

6 spring onions, finely shredded

1 tablespoon sesame oil

2 garlic cloves, sliced

boiled rice, to serve

green beans sprinkled with
toasted sesame seeds, to serve

1 Rub the trout on both sides with the shredded ginger, then sprinkle over half of the soy sauce and spring onions and set aside for 10 minutes. Place the fillets on a heatproof plate, over-lapping them slightly.

2 Fill a steamer or large pan with 7.5 cm/3 in hot water and bring to a simmer. Place fish on plate on rack of steamer or on top of pan. Cover and steam gently for 15 minutes or until just tender.

3 Meanwhile, heat the oil and gently fry the garlic until golden brown. Remove the fish from the steamer and discard the juices, then transfer to serving plates and sprinkle over the remaining soy sauce and spring onions. Scatter the garlic over the trout and serve at once with boiled rice and green beans.

- *Per serving: calories 481, fat medium, saturated fat low, protein high, fibre medium, sodium medium*

American crispy salad

- **Total time: 25 minutes**
- **Budget • Serves 4**

---

3 slices day-old white bread, crusts removed and cut into 1 cm/½ in cubes

5 tablespoons olive oil

1 garlic clove, crushed

3 tablespoons grated Parmesan

1 tablespoon white wine vinegar

1 tablespoon wholegrain mustard

½ teaspoon caster sugar

1 teaspoon Worcestershire sauce

1 Cos lettuce

50 g/2 oz can anchovy fillets, drained and chopped

---

1 Preheat the oven to 200°C/400°F/Gas 6. Place the bread cubes in a bowl, add two tablespoons of the olive oil, the garlic and half of the Parmesan and toss well to coat. Spread on a baking sheet and bake for about 10 minutes until golden.

2 Make the dressing: place the vinegar, mustard, sugar and seasoning in a bowl and whisk with an electric beater until the mixture has thickened. Add the remaining olive oil and Worcestershire sauce and whisk until smooth.

3 Tear the lettuce into large pieces and place in a salad bowl. Pour over the dressing and toss well to coat. Add the remaining Parmesan and anchovies; season to taste. Toss well, scatter over the croûtons and serve at once.

- *Per serving: calories 310, fat high, saturated fat medium, protein medium, fibre low, sodium high*

Tuna rice cakes

- Total time: 25 minutes
- Budget ● Serves 4

75 g/3 oz basmati rice

200 g/7 oz can tuna in brine, drained

4 spring onions, finely chopped

50 g/2 oz cashew nuts, chopped

1 tablespoon light soy sauce

1 egg, beaten

1 tablespoon sunflower oil

200 g/7 oz can chopped tomatoes

seasoning

mixed salad leaves, to serve

1 Cook the rice in boiling salted water for 10 minutes until just tender; rinse and drain well. Place in a bowl with the tuna, most of the spring onions, the cashew nuts, soy sauce and egg and mix until well combined.

2 Mould the mixture into eight small patties. Heat the oil in a large frying pan and fry the patties for 3–4 minutes on each side until golden.

3 Meanwhile, mix the tomatoes with the rest of the onions and season. Heat gently and serve with the rice cakes and salad.

● *Per serving: calories 227, fat medium, saturated fat medium, protein high, fibre medium, sodium high*

Mixed fried rice

- Total time: 25 minutes
- Average ● Serves 4

225 g/8 oz long grain white rice
2 tablespoons vegetable oil
1 garlic clove, crushed
1 teaspoon crushed fresh root ginger (optional)
175 g/6 oz cooked peeled prawns
100 g/4 oz frozen sweetcorn
75 g/3 oz frozen sliced green beans, thawed
50 g/2 oz salted cashew nuts
1 tablespoon light soy sauce
6 spring onions, thinly sliced diagonally
1 teaspoon sesame oil
seasoning

① Cook the rice in a large pan of boiling salted water for 10–12 minutes until almost tender. Drain and rinse with boiling water. Spread out on a large tray and leave to cool slightly.

② Shortly before serving, heat the oil in a wok or large frying pan. Add the garlic and ginger and stir-fry for 2 minutes. Stir in the prawns, sweetcorn and beans and fry for 1 minute.

③ Add the cashews and rice and stir-fry for 3 minutes. Stir in the soy sauce, spring onions and seasoning. Sprinkle with the sesame oil and serve.

● *Per serving: calories 444, fat medium, saturated fat low, protein medium, fibre low, sodium medium*

Tuna with pasta quills

- Total time: 25 minutes
- Budget ● Serves 4–6

350 g/12 oz pasta quills	225 g/8 oz can tuna in oil, drained and flaked
2 tablespoons olive oil	
1 onion, chopped	100 g/4 oz Cheddar, finely grated
2 garlic cloves, crushed	
2 x 400 g/14 oz cans chopped tomatoes	3 tablespoons fresh white breadcrumbs
1 tablespoon tomato purée	seasoning
50 g/2 oz pitted black olives, quartered	leafy salad, to serve
1 tablespoon chopped fresh oregano or 1 teaspoon dried oregano	

1 Cook pasta in boiling salted water until *al dente*. Meanwhile, heat the oil and fry the onion and garlic until softened. Add the tomatoes, tomato purée, olives, oregano and seasoning. Simmer gently for 5 minutes.

2 Drain the pasta and toss well in the tomato mixture. Stir in the tuna, spoon into a flameproof dish and sprinkle over cheese and breadcrumbs. Grill for about 10 minutes until the pasta is heated through and the cheese is bubbling. Serve with salad.

● *Per serving: calories 448, fat medium, saturated fat medium, protein medium, fibre medium, sodium medium*

Stuffed spinach mackerel

- Total time: 35 minutes
- Cheap ● Serves 4

4 whole mackerel, about 175 g/6 oz each, cleaned	50 g/2 oz dried white breadcrumbs
25 g/1 oz butter	good pinch of freshly grated nutmeg
1 onion, finely chopped	
2 garlic cloves, crushed	seasoning
225 g/8 oz fresh spinach	lemon wedges and flatleaf parsley sprigs, to garnish
2–3 tablespoons freshly grated Parmesan	new potatoes, to serve

❶ Preheat the oven to 190°C/375°F/Gas 5. Slash the mackerel four times. Melt the butter and fry the onion and garlic for about 10 minutes until golden.

❷ Place the spinach in a pan with a pinch of salt and just the water that clings to the leaves after washing them. Cover and cook for about 5 minutes until tender. Drain and roughly chop.

❸ Tip the spinach into a bowl and add the onion and garlic, Parmesan, breadcrumbs and nutmeg. Mix together, then season to taste.

❹ Open out the four mackerel and divide the stuffing among them, pressing down well. Fold over the backbone to enclose the stuffing.

❺ Arrange in a lightly oiled, shallow baking dish and bake for 20 minutes. Garnish with lemon wedges and parsley and serve with new potatoes.

- *Per serving: calories 823, fat medium, saturated fat medium, protein high, fibre medium, sodium medium*

Potato and tuna salad

- **Total time: 20 minutes**
- **Average ● Serves 4**

450 g/1 lb small new potatoes	**200 g/7 oz can tuna in oil, drained and flaked**
100 g/4 oz cherry tomatoes, halved	**50 g/2 oz can anchovy fillets, drained**
3 eggs	
175 g/6 oz French beans, tops removed	**50 g/2 oz black olives, halved and stoned**
6 tablespoons olive oil	**seasoning**
2 tablespoons red wine vinegar	**crusty bread, to serve**
1 tablespoon wholegrain mustard	

1 Cook the potatoes in boiling salted water for 8–10 minutes or until tender; drain. Season the tomatoes and grill for 2 minutes.

2 Boil the eggs for 4–5 minutes, shell and cut into quarters. Cook the beans in boiling salted water for 2–3 minutes. Drain and refresh in cold water.

3 Mix the olive oil, vinegar, mustard and seasoning in a small bowl until well blended.

4 Put the potatoes, tomatoes, eggs and beans in a salad bowl; scatter over the tuna, anchovies and olives. Toss lightly with the dressing. Serve warm or cold with crusty bread.

- *Per serving: calories 686, fat high, saturated fat medium, protein medium, fibre medium, sodium high*

Spicy vegetable curry

- **Total time: 35 minutes**
- **Budget ● Serves 4–6**

2 tablespoons vegetable oil
2 tablespoons mild curry paste
2 garlic cloves, crushed
2 potatoes, chopped
3 carrots, sliced diagonally
1 green pepper, seeded and chopped
300 ml/½ pint vegetable stock
1 small cauliflower, cut into small florets
400 g/14 oz can chick peas, drained
2 tablespoons tomato chutney
150 g/5 oz natural yogurt
seasoning
boiled rice, to serve

1 Heat the oil in a large pan, add the curry paste and garlic and fry for 2–3 minutes, stirring continuously.

2 Add potatoes, carrots and pepper and coat in the oil. Add stock, bring to the boil. Cover and simmer for 10 minutes.

3 Add cauliflower and chick peas and stir well. Simmer for 10–15 minutes until vegetables are soft, then add the chutney, most of the yogurt and the seasoning. Drizzle over reserved yogurt and serve with rice.

- *Per serving: calories 415, fat medium, saturated fat low, protein medium, fibre high, sodium medium*

Pasta and feta cheese salad

- ● Total time: 25 minutes
- ● Budget ● Serves 4

175 g/6 oz tricolour fusilli
(pasta spirals)

1 red pepper, seeded and
quartered

4 tablespoons lemon juice

1 tablespoon clear honey

1 teaspoon dry English mustard

1 teaspoon ground paprika

100 g/4 oz sugar snap peas

100 g/4 oz cauliflower florets,
thinly sliced

100 g/4 oz feta cheese, cubed

50 g/2 oz black olives

seasoning

1 Cook the pasta in plenty of boiling salted water for 8–10 minutes. Drain and refresh under cold running water, then set aside.

2 Grill the pepper, skin side up, until the skin is blistered and charred. Cool slightly, then peel off the skin and cut the flesh into strips.

3 Place the lemon juice, honey, mustard, paprika and seasoning in a screw-topped jar and shake until thoroughly mixed.

4 Mix together the cooked pasta, pepper strips, sugar snap peas, cauliflower and feta cheese. Stir in the dressing until the vegetables and cheese are well coated. Scatter over the olives and serve.

- ● *Per serving: calories 264, fat medium, saturated fat medium, protein medium, fibre high, sodium high*

Lentil hot pot

- Total time: 30 minutes
- Budget • Serves 4

1 tablespoon olive oil
1 onion, chopped
1 garlic clove, crushed
2 potatoes, peeled and diced
2 carrots, finely chopped
2 celery sticks, chopped
225 g/8 oz red lentils
400 g/14 oz can chopped tomatoes
2 tablespoons tomato purée
1 bay leaf
½ teaspoon dried oregano
1 vegetable stock cube
seasoning
pitta bread, to serve

1 Heat oil in a large pan and fry onion and garlic until onion well softened. Add potatoes, carrots, celery sticks and lentils; fry for 1–2 minutes, stirring occasionally.

2 Add tomatoes, tomato purée, bay leaf and oregano; season to taste. Crumble in the stock cube and stir in 450 ml/¾ pint water.

3 Bring to the boil and simmer for 25–30 minutes or until the lentils are tender. Ladle into warmed bowls and serve with the warmed pitta bread.

- *Per serving: calories 486, fat medium, saturated fat low, protein high, fibre high, sodium medium*

Tricolour fettuccine with herb sauce

- **Total time: 25 minutes**
- **Budget ● Serves 4**

350 g/12 oz tricolour fettuccine

4 tablespoons olive oil

25 g/1 oz butter

1 teaspoon grated lemon rind

50 g/2 oz fresh herbs, such as parsley, basil, coriander and chives, chopped

4 tomatoes, peeled, seeded and chopped

seasoning

freshly grated Parmesan, to serve

1 Bring a large pan of salted water to the boil and cook the fettuccine for 10 minutes, or according to the manufacturer's instructions, until *al dente*.

2 Meanwhile, heat the olive oil and butter in a frying pan until the butter has just melted. Add the lemon rind and seasoning, then stir in the herbs and chopped tomatoes.

3 When the pasta is ready, drain and rinse in boiling water and turn out into a warmed serving bowl. Pour over the sauce and toss the pasta to coat thoroughly. Serve at once with the Parmesan.

● *Per serving: calories 453, fat medium, saturated fat medium, protein medium, fibre medium, sodium low*

Courgette and tomato tart

- **Total time: 40 minutes**
- **Budget** ● **Serves 4**

---

2 tablespoons olive oil

2 onions, sliced

1 tablespoon caster sugar

3 large tomatoes, thinly sliced

1 courgette, thinly sliced

2 teaspoons chopped fresh oregano or 1 teaspoon dried

175 g/6 oz ready-made shortcrust pastry

seasoning

fresh oregano leaves, to garnish (optional)

---

① Preheat the oven to 200°C/400°F/Gas 6. Heat the oil in a heavy-based pan and fry the onions for about 5 minutes until flecked with brown. Sprinkle with sugar and stir for 1 minute, then add 3 tablespoons of water and simmer until tender.

② Spoon the onion mixture into a shallow 20 cm/8 in round sandwich tin. Arrange the tomatoes and courgette in an overlapping layer. Season and sprinkle over the oregano.

③ Roll out the pastry to a 25 cm/10 in round and place over the vegetables, tucking the edges down the side of the tin. Trim, place on a baking sheet and bake for 20–25 minutes or until the pastry is deep brown. Turn out on to a serving dish, scatter over the oregano leaves, if using, and serve hot or warm.

● *Per serving: calories 307, fat high, saturated fat high, protein low, fibre medium, solution medium*

Roasted vegetable pasta

- **Total time: 40 minutes**
- **Budget ● Serves 4**

3 carrots, cut into strips
3 celery sticks, cut into strips
1 parsnip, cut into strips
2 beefsteak tomatoes, halved
4 small garlic cloves, halved
3 tablespoons olive oil
450 g/1 lb penne (tubes)
3 tablespoons freshly grated Parmesan
5 tablespoons chopped fresh parsley
seasoning
Parmesan shavings, to garnish

1 Preheat the oven to 200°C/400°F/Gas 6. Place all of the vegetables (and the garlic halves) in a roasting tin. Pour over the oil, season and toss lightly. Roast for 30 minutes until lightly browned. Once cooked, scoop out the flesh from the tomatoes and discard the skin.

2 Meanwhile, cook the pasta in a pan of boiling salted water for 10 minutes or until *al dente*. Drain and stir in the vegetables with Parmesan and parsley. Garnish with Parmesan shavings and serve at once.

● *Per serving: calories 587, fat medium, saturated fat medium, protein medium, fibre high, sodium low*

Broccoli and walnut spaghetti

- Total time: 20 minutes
- Budget • Serves 4

3 tablespoons olive oil
2 garlic cloves, crushed
100 g/4 oz fresh white breadcrumbs
350 g/12 oz spaghetti
350 g/12 oz broccoli florets
25 g/1 oz walnuts, toasted and roughly chopped
seasoning

1 Heat one tablespoon of the oil in a large frying pan and gently fry the garlic for 1 minute. Add breadcrumbs and seasoning and fry until crisp and golden.

2 Bring a pan of salted water to the boil and cook the spaghetti for about 10–12 minutes or until *al dente*. Meanwhile, cook broccoli in a little boiling, salted water or steam until just tender.

3 Drain the spaghetti and toss in the remaining oil. Tip in the broccoli and breadcrumb mixture and toss until combined. Divide among serving plates, scatter over the walnuts and serve immediately.

● *Per serving: calories 534, fat medium, saturated fat low, protein medium, fibre medium, sodium low*

Leek and mushroom pie

- Total time: 40 minutes
- Cheap • Serves 6

| 1 tablespoon olive oil |
| 4 small leeks, cut into 1 cm/ ½ in pieces |
| 1 red pepper, seeded and chopped |
| 225 g/8 oz mushrooms, sliced |
| 450 g/1 lb puff pastry, thawed if frozen |
| 2 teaspoons Dijon mustard |
| 175 g/6 oz Cheshire cheese, crumbled |
| 1 teaspoon chopped fresh thyme or ½ teaspoon dried |
| 1 egg, beaten, to glaze |
| seasoning |

1 Preheat the oven to 200°C/400°F/Gas 6. Heat the oil in a frying pan and fry the leeks, pepper and mushrooms over a high heat for 2–3 minutes. Leave to cool a little, tip off any excess moisture and season.

2 Roll out half of the pastry on a floured board to a 25 cm/10 in square and transfer to a greased baking sheet; spread with the mustard. Roll out the rest of the pastry to a 30 cm/12 in square.

3 Spoon leek mixture into centre of pastry; scatter over cheese and thyme. Brush edges with cold water, place reserved pastry on top and crimp edges together. Make slits in pastry, brush with egg, then bake for 25–30 minutes until golden.

- *Per serving: calories 452, fat high, saturated fat medium, protein medium, fibre medium, sodium medium*

Cauliflower and potato curry

- Total time: 40 minutes
- Budget ● Serves 4

4 tablespoons vegetable oil
1 large onion, finely sliced
2 garlic cloves, finely sliced
1 teaspoon grated fresh root ginger
450 g/1 lb potatoes, cut into bite-sized pieces
1 small cauliflower head, broken into florets
½ teaspoon black mustard seeds
2 tablespoons hot curry paste
100 g/4 oz frozen peas
juice of 1 lemon
seasoning
naan bread, to serve

1 Heat half of the oil and fry half of the onion, the garlic and ginger until golden. Add the potatoes and cauliflower and fry gently for 3–4 minutes. Add half of the mustard seeds and cook until they start popping.

2 Stir in the curry paste and 750 ml/1¼ pints water. Simmer for about 20 minutes until the liquid has reduced by half.

3 Add peas and seasoning. Cook, uncovered, for 4–5 minutes, sprinkle with lemon juice and leave for 5 minutes.

4 Meanwhile, fry remaining onion in remaining oil until crisp. Add the rest of the mustard seeds and cook until they start to pop. Sprinkle over the curry and serve with the naan bread.

● *Per serving: calories 520, fat medium, saturated fat low, protein medium, fibre medium, sodium medium*

Summer salad bowl

- Total time: 30 minutes
- Budget ● Serves 4–6

| 225 g/8 oz new potatoes, cooked and sliced |
| 225 g/8 oz cauliflower, cut into tiny florets |
| 2 large carrots, grated |
| 175 g/6 oz peas, cooked |
| 100 g/4 oz radishes, sliced |
| 100 g/4 oz lettuce, shredded |
| FOR THE DRESSING |
| 2 tablespoons olive oil |
| 1 tablespoon fresh lemon juice |
| 2 tablespoons snipped fresh chives |
| 2 tablespoons wholegrain mustard |
| seasoning |

1 Make the dressing: place oil, lemon juice, chives, mustard and seasoning in a screw-topped jar; shake well.

2 Arrange vegetables in layers in a serving dish, preferably glass. Start with the potatoes, then cauliflower, carrots, peas and radishes, drizzling dressing between layers.

3 Sprinkle lettuce and any remaining dressing on top. Chill and serve with crusty bread.

- *Per serving: calories 177, fat medium, saturated fat low, protein medium, fibre high, sodium high*

Mushroom risotto

- ● Total time: 35 minutes
- ● Cheap ● Serves 4

75 g/3 oz butter	1 litre/1¾ pints vegetable stock
1 onion, finely chopped	
350 g/12 oz mushrooms, such as chestnut, cep, shiitake, sliced	50 g/2 oz Parmesan, grated
	4 tablespoons chopped fresh parsley
300 g/10 oz arborio or risotto rice	seasoning
	Parmesan shavings, to garnish

❶ Heat 50 g/2 oz of the butter in a large pan and gently fry the onion for about 5 minutes until softened. Add the mushrooms and fry for 2–3 minutes.

❷ Stir in rice, then add a ladle of stock, bring to the boil and simmer until stock is absorbed; add another ladle of stock.

❸ Simmer gently for about 20 minutes, stirring continuously. Add another ladle or two of stock each time the liquid has been absorbed into the rice.

❹ Stir in remaining butter, grated Parmesan, parsley and seasoning. Cover and leave to rest for 5 minutes before serving. Garnish with Parmesan shavings.

● *Per serving: calories 509, fat medium, saturated fat high, protein medium, fibre medium, sodium medium*

Egg and spinach brunch

- **Total time: 35 minutes**
- **Budget** ● **Serves 2**

2 tablespoons olive oil
2 potatoes, cut into chunks
1 onion, cut into wedges
50 g/2 oz frozen leaf spinach, thawed
1 teaspoon chopped fresh thyme or ½ teaspoon dried thyme
2 eggs
25 g/1 oz Cheddar, grated
seasoning

1 Preheat the oven to 200°C/400°F/Gas 6. Heat the oil in an ovenproof dish, add the potatoes and onion and toss to coat. Bake for 20–25 minutes until lightly golden.

2 Gently squeeze out the excess water from the spinach. Remove the dish from the oven and mix in the spinach, thyme and seasoning, then carefully break in the eggs.

3 Sprinkle Cheddar over the top, then season and bake for about 10 minutes until the eggs are lightly set. Serve at once.

● *Per serving: calories 359, fat high, saturated fat high, protein medium, fibre medium, sodium medium*

Sardine, cheese and tomato toasties

- **Total time: 20 minutes**
- **Budget ● Serves 4**

4 slices thick-cut white bread
margarine or butter, for spreading
6 tomatoes, sliced
freshly ground black pepper
handful of fresh basil leaves, roughly torn
175 g/6 oz mature Cheddar, thinly sliced
120 g/4½ oz can sardines in oil, drained
fresh basil sprigs, to garnish

1 Lightly toast the bread on both sides and spread with the margarine or butter. Arrange the tomato slices on the toast so they overlap, then season generously with freshly ground black pepper and scatter over the basil.

2 Divide the cheese among the slices of toast and place under a medium grill for 1–2 minutes until the cheese starts to bubble. Halve the sardines lengthways and arrange two pieces on top of each toastie.

3 Place the toasties under the grill for a further minute until they are golden brown and bubbling. Season generously with freshly ground black pepper and garnish with basil sprigs. Serve immediately.

● *Per serving: calories 485, fat high, saturated fat high, protein high, fibre medium, sodium high*

Smoked trout pâté

- Total time: 20 minutes
- Average ● Serves 4

225 g/8 oz smoked trout fillet,
skinned and boned

2 tablespoons melted butter

50 g/2 oz fromage frais or
cream cheese

a little lemon juice

1 tablespoon creamed
horseradish sauce

freshly ground black pepper

4 slices medium sliced white
bread

flatleaf parsley sprigs, to
garnish

halved cherry tomatoes, to
serve

1 Place the smoked trout, butter, fromage frais or cream cheese, lemon juice, creamed horseradish and ground black pepper in a liquidiser or food processor and blend until smooth. Spoon into a serving dish and smooth firmly; cover and chill until ready to use.

2 Meanwhile, toast the bread on both sides. Cut off the crusts then, holding the toast flat, slide the knife between the toasted edges to split the bread.

3 Cut each piece of bread into four triangles and grill, untoasted side up, until golden brown and the edges curl. To serve, divide the pâté among plates, garnish with the parsley and serve with the toast and tomatoes.

- *Per serving: calories 240, fat medium, saturated fat high, protein high, fibre medium, sodium medium*

Smoked mackerel toasts

- Total time: 20 minutes
- Budget • Serves 4

225 g/8 oz smoked mackerel
4 tablespoons natural yogurt
2 tablespoons creamed horseradish sauce
4 spring onions
1 crusty wholemeal loaf
4 tomatoes, sliced
seasoning

1. Skin the mackerel and discard the skin and bones; mash the flesh in a bowl. Add the yogurt and horseradish sauce; season to taste and mix well. Snip in the white part of the spring onions and retain the rest.

2. Cut the loaf into 16 slices, discarding end pieces. Toast on both sides and place two slices on each serving plate. Arrange tomatoes on top of each slice, then spoon over the mackerel mixture. Snip over the remaining spring onions, then cover with another slice of toast and serve.

- *Per serving: calories 428, fat medium, saturated fat medium, protein medium, fibre high, sodium high*

Speedy pizzas

- Total time: 30 minutes
- Budget • Serves 4

150 g/5 oz packet pizza base mix
½ teaspoon dried oregano
1 tablespoon olive oil
1 large onion, halved and thinly sliced
2 garlic cloves, finely chopped
6 tomatoes, sliced
1 courgette, pared into ribbons
100 g/4 oz Cheddar, cubed
seasoning

1 Preheat the oven to 220°C/425°F/Gas 7. Empty the entire contents of the packet pizza base mix into a bowl, stir in the oregano and make it up according to the instructions on the packet.

2 Divide the dough into four pieces and roll out each one into a 15 cm/6 in circle. Place well apart on two greased baking sheets.

3 Heat the olive oil in a frying pan and fry the onions and garlic until the onions are lightly browned.

4 Arrange the tomato slices evenly on the pizza bases and scatter the onion and garlic mixture on top.

5 Arrange the courgette ribbons and Cheddar over the onion mixture and season. Bake for 15–20 minutes until golden and bubbling.

- *Per serving: calories 297, fat medium, saturated fat high, protein medium, fibre medium, sodium medium*

Hot kipper toasts

- **Total time: 25 minutes**
- **Budget** ● **Serves 2**

1 boil-in-the-bag whole kipper
50 g/2 oz Cheddar, grated
3 tablespoons fromage frais or thick Greek yogurt
dash of Worcestershire sauce
½ ciabatta loaf, cut into slices
lime wedges, to serve

❶ Place the kipper in a pan of boiling water and cook according to the instructions on the packet. Remove from the pan, cool, then remove from the bag. Skin and mash the kipper.

❷ Add the Cheddar, fromage frais (or thick Greek yogurt) and a dash of Worcestershire sauce to the kipper and mix well.

❸ Toast the ciabatta, then spread over the kipper mixture. Grill until bubbling, squeeze over a little lime juice, if desired, and serve at once.

● *Per serving: calories 431, fat medium, saturated fat high, protein high, fibre medium, sodium high*

Sweetcorn salsa with tortilla chips

- Total time: 10 minutes
- Budget • Serves 2

| 50 g/2 oz sweetcorn, fresh or thawed, if frozen |
| 100 g/4 oz packet tortilla chips |
| 1 tomato, chopped |
| 2 spring onions, finely chopped |
| 2 tablespoons chopped fresh coriander (optional) |
| 3 tablespoons soured cream |
| 25 g/1 oz Cheddar, grated |
| a little cayenne pepper |
| seasoning |

1 If you are using fresh corn, place in a pan with two tablespoons of cold water, cover and cook for 5 minutes or until just tender.

2 Pile the tortilla chips into a bowl and scatter the sweetcorn, tomato, spring onions and coriander, if using, on top. Spoon over the soured cream; season.

3 Sprinkle over the Cheddar and season with cayenne pepper. Grill for 2–3 minutes until the Cheddar melts. Serve hot.

- *Per serving: calories 354, fat high, saturated fat medium, protein medium, fibre medium, sodium high*

Bruschetta with chorizo sausage and tomatoes

- Total time: 20 minutes
- Cheap ● Serves 4

2 tablespoons olive oil

1 onion, halved and sliced

1 yellow pepper, seeded and sliced

225 g/8 oz chorizo sausage, sliced

225 g/8 oz cherry tomatoes, halved

4 large slices fresh bread

1 garlic clove, halved

seasoning

1 Heat half of the oil in a large frying pan and fry the onion and pepper for 3–4 minutes until softened.

2 Add the chorizo and fry for 2–3 minutes until it is sizzling and beginning to brown, stirring occasionally. Add the tomatoes and seasoning and fry for another 5 minutes until the tomato skins are beginning to split.

3 Meanwhile, grill the bread until crisp. Rub the garlic clove all over one side of each slice of toasted bread, then carefully drizzle over the remaining olive oil. Pile the chorizo mixture on top and serve immediately.

● *Per serving: calories 480, fat high, saturated fat high, protein medium, fibre medium, sodium high*

Croque monsieur

- **Total time: 15 minutes**
- **Budget ● Serves 4**

8 thin bread slices, crusts removed	**50 g/2 oz butter or margarine, melted**
4 teaspoons wholegrain mustard	**fresh parsley sprigs, to garnish**
175 g/6 oz Cheddar, sliced	
175 g/6 oz wafer-thin ham slices	

1 Spread half of the bread slices on one side with the mustard; cover with a layer of Cheddar. Arrange a couple of layers of ham on top of each and finish with the remaining cheese and bread. Press down lightly to make the sandwiches.

2 Brush the sandwiches all over with the melted butter or margarine and grill for 3–5 minutes on each side until they are lightly browned. Cut in half, garnish with parsley and serve.

● *Per serving: calories 444, fat high, saturated fat high, protein medium, fibre low, sodium high*

Mushrooms and pesto with garlic bread

- Total time: 30 minutes
- Cheap ● Serves 4

8 large cup mushrooms	FOR THE GARLIC BREAD
8 teaspoons ready-made pesto sauce	1 small French baguette
	50 g/2 oz butter
25 g/1 oz fresh white breadcrumbs	2 garlic cloves, finely chopped
	seasoning
25 g/1 oz Parmesan, freshly grated	fresh basil leaves, to garnish (optional)

1 Preheat the oven to 180°C/350°F/Gas 4. Make the garlic bread: slice the French baguette diagonally to within 1 cm/½ in of the base. Melt the butter in a pan, add the garlic and gently fry for 1–2 minutes. Brush each slice with the butter mixture, wrap in foil and bake for 15 minutes.

2 Meanwhile, arrange the mushrooms on a lightly oiled baking sheet and spoon a teaspoon of pesto on each one. Mix together the breadcrumbs, Parmesan and seasoning and sprinkle on top. Bake for 10–15 minutes or until golden. Garnish with basil leaves (if using) and serve with the garlic bread.

- *Per serving: calories 137, fat high, saturated fat high, protein medium, fibre medium, sodium medium*

Satsuma and raisin tart

- Total time: 40 minutes
- Cheap ● Serves 4–6

225 g/8 oz shortcrust pastry,
thawed if frozen

175 g/6 oz raisins

2 tablespoons light muscovado
sugar

4 satsumas

2 bananas, mashed

50 g/2 oz ground almonds

beaten egg or milk, to glaze

175 g/6 oz thick Greek yogurt,
to serve

① Preheat the oven to 200°C/400°F/Gas 6. Set aside a quarter of the pastry and roll out rest on a floured board into a round larger than a 20 cm/8 in pie dish. Line the pie dish and trim the edges.

② Mix together raisins and sugar. Peel and segment satsumas over the raisin mixture to catch any juices, then cut into pieces. Stir the satsumas into the raisin mixture with the bananas and ground almonds, then spoon into the pastry-lined dish; level the surface.

③ Roll out the reserved dough into a 23 cm/9 in long strip and cut it lengthways into narrow strips. Arrange the strips over the filling to form a lattice pattern, sticking down the ends with a little water. Brush the dough with beaten egg or milk and bake for about 25 minutes until just set. Serve either warm or cold, cut into wedges and topped with a generous dollop of Greek yogurt.

● *Per serving: calories 363, fat medium, saturated fat medium, protein low, fibre medium, sodium medium*

Summer fruit sabayon

- Total time: 25 minutes
- Cheap ● Serves 4

2 egg yolks, beaten
50 g/2 oz caster sugar
grated rind of ½ lemon
150 ml/¼ pint dry white wine
4 tablespoons single cream
450 g/1 lb mixed summer fruit,
such as blueberries,
raspberries, stoned cherries,
grapes and apricot wedges

1 Place the egg yolks and sugar in a heatproof bowl and beat until well combined. Add the lemon rind and wine, then set the bowl over a pan of simmering water (do not allow the bowl to touch the water).

2 Continue beating until the sabayon is smooth and has thickened, then gradually stir in the cream. Whisk for 1 minute until well combined.

3 Arrange the fruit in a shallow ovenproof dish, pour over the sabayon and place under a hot grill until bubbling and golden. Serve at once.

● *Per serving: calories 182, fat medium, saturated fat medium, protein low, fibre medium, sodium low*

Almond tartlets with apricots and raspberries

- Total time: 35 minutes
- Average • Serves 4

65 g/2½ oz butter, softened, plus extra for greasing

50 g/2 oz golden caster sugar

50 g/2 oz ground almonds

175 g/6 oz Greek strained yogurt

3 fresh apricots, peeled, stoned and quartered

24 fresh raspberries

12 mint sprigs, to decorate

1 Preheat the oven to 180°C/350°F/Gas 4. Beat the butter and sugar with a wooden spoon or electric mixer for 2–3 minutes until light and fluffy, then beat in the ground almonds. Divide the mixture among 12–14 lightly buttered bun tins and bake in the oven for 15–20 minutes or until golden brown.

2 Remove the tartlets from the oven and leave them in their tins for about 5 minutes before turning out carefully. Cool on a wire rack.

3 Place a small dollop of Greek strained yogurt in the centre of each tartlet, then arrange the apricots and raspberries on top. Decorate with the mint sprigs.

- *Per serving: calories 184, fat high, saturated fat high, protein low, fibre medium, sodium low*

Flambéed pineapple

● **Total time: 25 minutes**
● **Average** ● **Serves 4**

1 kg/2 lb fresh pineapple,
peeled

50 g/2 oz pecan nut halves

50 g/2 oz butter

75 g/3 oz light muscovado
sugar

6 tablespoons light rum

vanilla ice-cream, to serve

❶ Cut the pineapple across into eight even slices and carefully remove the cores with a pastry cutter to make rings.

❷ Evenly space the pecans on a baking sheet and grill for about 5 minutes, turning occasionally, until toasted. Leave to cool.

❸ Melt the butter in a large frying pan and stir in the sugar. Cook gently for 2 minutes until the sugar has dissolved. Add the pineapple rings and cook for 4–5 minutes, turning once, until they are tender. Scatter the pecan nuts into the pan and pour over the rum. Bring to boil, hold a lighted match to side of pan and set the rum alight.

❹ Baste the fruit with the sauce using a long-handled spoon for 1–2 minutes until the flames have died down. Serve immediately with scoops of vanilla ice-cream.

● *Per serving: calories 573, fat medium, saturated fat high, protein low, fibre medium, sodium low*

Apricot pudding

- Total time: 35 minutes
- Budget ● Serves 6

2 eggs, separated

50 g/2 oz golden caster sugar

1 teaspoon vanilla essence

25 g/1 oz ground almonds

2 tablespoons double cream

50 ml/2 fl oz milk

2 x 400 g/14 oz cans apricot halves, drained

icing sugar, for dusting

fromage frais, to serve

❶ Preheat the oven to 200°C/400°F/Gas 6. Beat together the egg yolks, sugar and vanilla essence in a large mixing bowl until foamy. Beat in the almonds, then the double cream and milk. Whisk the egg whites very lightly in a separate bowl until they just begin to hold their shape, then carefully fold into the egg and sugar mixture.

❷ Pour the mixture into a buttered, shallow ovenproof dish and arrange the apricots, round sides up, on top. Bake for 25 minutes or until just set. You may need to cover the pudding with foil towards the end of the cooking time to prevent it turning too brown. Dust with icing sugar and serve hot with a dollop of fromage frais.

- *Per serving: calories 182, fat medium, saturated fat high, protein medium, fibre medium, sodium low*

Mixed berry pie

● **Total time: 35 minutes**
● **Average** ● **Serves 4**

75 g/3 oz porridge oats
150 g/5 oz desiccated coconut
120 g/4½ oz butter, softened
FOR THE FILLING
3 tablespoons plain flour
pinch of salt
50 g/2 oz caster sugar
3 egg yolks
300 ml/½ pint milk
grated rind of 1 lemon
3 tablespoons thick double cream
350 g/12 oz mixed soft berries (strawberries, raspberries, redcurrants and blackberries)

1 Preheat the oven to 150°C/300°F/Gas 2. Mix together oats, coconut and butter and press firmly into the base and sides of a 20 cm/8 in loose-bottomed flat tin. Bake for 15 minutes; cool.

2 Sift the flour and salt into a bowl. Beat sugar and egg yolks together until thick and creamy, then gradually mix in the flour.

3 Heat the milk and lemon rind in a small pan, bring to simmering point, cool slightly then pour into the yolks, stirring constantly. Tip into a small pan and bring to the boil. Cook, stirring constantly until thickened; about 2 minutes.

4 Cool, stirring occasionally to prevent a skin forming. Fold in the cream and pour into the pie case. Pile the berries on top. Chill and serve with cream.

● *Per serving: calories 746, fat high, saturated fat high, protein low, fibre high, sodium medium*

Raspberry swirl

- Total time: 25 minutes
- Cheap ● Serves 4

4 Amaretti biscuits, roughly chopped
175 g/6 oz raspberries
3 tablespoons clear honey
150 ml/¼ pint double cream
150 ml/¼ pint fromage frais
flaked almonds, to decorate
mint sprigs, to decorate

1 Divide most of the Amaretti biscuits among four stemmed glasses and top each one with a couple of raspberries. Blend the honey and remaining raspberries in a food processor or liquidiser until you have a smooth purée.

2 Whip the cream until it is just beginning to hold its shape, then fold in the fromage frais. Using a metal spoon, lightly fold the raspberry purée into the cream mixture to give a swirled effect. Spoon carefully into the glasses.

3 Spread out the flaked almonds on aluminium foil, then place under the grill and lightly toast. When they have cooled, sprinkle the almonds over the cream mixture and chill until ready to serve. Before serving, decorate with the mint.

- *Per serving: calories 339, fat high, saturated fat high, protein low, fibre medium, sodium low*

Caramelised apples

- **Total time: 20 minutes**
- **Budget** • **Serves 4**

---

1 orange

---

4 dessert apples, halved, cored and cut into thick wedges

---

squeeze of lemon juice

---

50 g/2 oz butter

---

2 tablespoons demerara sugar

---

thick Greek yogurt and ground cinnamon, to serve (optional)

---

1 Using a zester, finely pare the rind from the orange into strips, then cut the orange in half and squeeze out the juice. Toss the apple wedges in the lemon juice to avoid any discoloration.

2 Heat the butter in a large frying pan, add the apple wedges and fry gently for about 5 minutes until they turn golden, making sure that they don't burn.

3 Sprinkle over the orange juice and sugar. Continue to cook for about 3 minutes until the apple wedges are glazed with sauce. Stir in the orange rind. Serve hot with yogurt and a sprinkling of cinnamon, if you wish.

• *Per serving: calories 200, fat high, saturated fat high, protein low, fibre high, sodium medium*

Spiced fruit parcels

- Total time: 25 minutes
- Cheap ● Serves 4

2 bananas
225 g/8 oz strawberries, hulled
2 firm nectarines or peaches
juice of 2 oranges
1 tablespoon brandy or rum
¼ teaspoon ground cinnamon
50 g/2 oz demerara sugar
50 g/2 oz flaked almonds,
toasted, to decorate
vanilla ice-cream, to serve

1 Preheat the oven to 200°C/400°F/Gas 6. Peel the bananas and cut into 1 cm/½ in slices. Halve the strawberries. Halve and stone the nectarines or peaches and cut into small wedges. Cut four 25 cm/ 10 in squares of aluminium foil and divide the fruit among them.

2 Turn up the edges of the foil to catch the liquid and drizzle over the orange juice and brandy or rum. Dust the fruit with the cinnamon and sprinkle the sugar on top.

3 Bring the edges together to seal the parcels, making sure you leave plenty of room for air. Bake for 10–15 minutes or until the fruit has softened (it should still retain its shape). Open each parcel, sprinkle over a few almonds and serve with a scoop of ice-cream.

● *Per serving: calories 345, fat medium, saturated fat medium, protein medium, fibre medium, sodium low*

Hot banana split

- **Total time: 30 minutes**
- **Budget** ● **Serves 4**

---

4 bananas, unpeeled

---

4 scoops vanilla or pecan-flavoured or butterscotch-flavoured ice-cream

---

4 teaspoons maple or golden syrup

---

2 tablespoons flaked almonds or chopped hazelnuts, toasted

---

① Preheat the oven to 200°C/400°F/Gas 6. Place bananas on a baking sheet and bake for 20–25 minutes until the skins are completely blackened. Alternatively, place them on a barbecue after the first heat has died down. Cook for 10–15 minutes, turning, until the skins have blackened.

② Place the bananas in individual dishes. Carefully split them down the middle and place a scoop of ice-cream on top of each one. Drizzle over the maple or golden syrup and scatter the almonds or hazelnuts on top. Serve at once.

● *Per serving: calories 272, fat medium, saturated fat medium, protein low, fibre medium, sodium low*

Sweet peach sandwiches

- Total time: 20 minutes
- Budget ● Serves 4

8 thick bread slices
2 x 400 g/14 oz cans peach
slices, drained
4 tablespoons caster sugar
2 teaspoons ground cinnamon
150 ml/¼ pint milk
2 eggs, lightly beaten
50 g/2 oz butter

1 Cut out circles from the bread using a large pastry cutter. Mash half of the peaches with one tablespoon of the sugar and half of the cinnamon. Divide the peach mixture among four circles of bread, spreading the mixture right out to the edges. Top with the remaining circles.

2 Mix together the milk, eggs and one tablespoon of sugar until well combined. Heat the butter in a large frying pan. Dip the peach sandwiches in the egg mixture and fry on both sides until golden brown.

3 Mix together the remaining sugar and cinnamon. Arrange the remaining peach slices on individual serving plates. Slice each peach sandwich in half, place on the plates and sprinkle over the cinnamon sugar.

- *Per serving: calories 460, fat medium, saturated fat high, protein medium, fibre medium, sodium medium*

Crunchy plum crumble

- Total time: 30 minutes
- Cheap ● Serves 6

10 plums
75 g/3 oz light muscovado sugar
FOR THE CRUMBLE
50 g/2 oz butter
100 g/4 oz plain flour
25 g/1 oz light muscovado sugar
75 g/3 oz crunchy muesli
vanilla ice-cream, to serve

① Preheat the oven to 200°C/400°F/Gas 6. Halve, stone and quarter the plums and tip into a 25 cm/10 in pie dish. Sprinkle over the sugar and toss well to coat the plums evenly.

② Make the crumble: rub the butter into the flour until the mixture resembles fine breadcrumbs, then stir in the sugar and muesli. Sprinkle the topping over the plums and bake for about 20 minutes or until golden brown. Serve hot with a scoop of vanilla ice-cream in each bowl.

● *Per serving: calories 376, fat medium, saturated fat high, protein low, fibre medium, sodium low*

Green fruit salad

- **Total time: 30 minutes**
- **Average ● Serves 4**

**1 small ogen or green
honeydew melon**

3 kiwi fruit, peeled

1 green-skinned pear

1 Granny Smith apple

**225 g/8 oz green seedless
grapes**

**200 ml/7 fl oz unsweetened
apple juice**

150 ml/¼ pint whipping cream

50 g/2 oz golden caster sugar

mint sprigs, to decorate

1 Scoop the flesh from the melon using a melon baller. Halve the kiwi fruit lengthways and cut into bite-size chunks.

2 Halve the pear and apple and scoop out the cores with a teaspoon, then cut into small chunks. Halve the grapes.

3 Spoon the fruit into individual glass bowls and pour over the apple juice. Whip the cream and place a dollop in each bowl.

4 Place the sugar and 4 tablespoons of water in a heavy-based pan and heat gently until the sugar dissolves. Brush water over the inside of the pan just above the syrup to wash the sugar crystals down, then boil gently until golden caramel in colour. Drizzle over the cream in the bowls and decorate with mint sprigs.

- *Per serving: calories 328, fat medium, saturated fat high, protein low, fibre high, sodium low*

Raspberry flapjacks

- Total time: 30 minutes
- Cheap ● Serves 4

50 g/2 oz butter
25 g/1 oz caster sugar
3 tablespoons golden syrup or honey
50 g/2 oz rolled oats
50 g/2 oz flaked almonds
1 teaspoon ground ginger
100 g/4 oz fromage frais
225 g/8 oz raspberries
icing sugar, to dust

1 Preheat the oven to 190°C/375°F/Gas 5. Melt the butter over a low heat. Add the sugar and syrup or honey and warm gently; do not boil. Remove from the heat and stir in the oats, almonds and ginger.

2 Drop mixture into eight small heaps on two parchment-lined baking sheets with enough room to spread. Flatten slightly; bake for 10–15 minutes until golden.

3 Remove from the oven and leave on the baking sheets for 5 minutes, then transfer to a wire rack to cool.

4 Spoon fromage frais on four of the flapjacks; scatter over raspberries. Top with the remaining flapjacks and dust with the icing sugar.

● *Per serving: calories 326, fat high, saturated fat high, protein medium, fibre medium, sodium low*

Pear and blackberry frangipane

- Total time: 40 minutes
- Cheap ● Serves 4–6

225 g/8 oz ready-made
shortcrust pastry

3 small ripe pears, peeled,
halved and cored

100 g/4 oz blackberries

50 g/2 oz soft margarine

50 g/2 oz caster sugar

50 g/2 oz ground almonds

25 g/1 oz plain flour

1 egg, beaten

25 g/1 oz flaked almonds

pouring cream, to serve

1 Preheat the oven to 200°C/400°F/Gas 6. Roll out the pastry on a lightly floured board and use to line a 23 cm/9 in flan tin.

2 Make several parallel cuts across the width of each pear half, without cutting right through. Arrange rounded sides up on top of the pastry. Scatter the blackberries on top.

3 Beat together the margarine, sugar, almonds, flour and egg for 1 minute. Spoon the mixture evenly around the pears, then sprinkle the almonds on top and bake for about 30 minutes until golden. Serve warm with cream.

● *Per serving: calories 606, fat high, saturated fat high, protein low, fibre medium, sodium high*

Baked apple meringue

- **Total time: 40 minutes**
- **Budget ● Serves 4**

2 large firm eating apples
4 tablespoons mincemeat
300 ml/½ pint apple juice
1 egg white
½ teaspoon ground cinnamon
50 g/2 oz caster sugar
15 g/½ oz flaked almonds
icing sugar, for dusting

1 Preheat the oven to 180°C/350°F/Gas 4. Halve the apples and scoop out the cores to make hollows. Fill with mincemeat and place in a baking dish. Pour the apple juice around the apples.

2 Whisk the egg white in a bowl until stiff, then gradually whisk in the cinnamon and sugar until the meringue is thick and glossy.

3 Top each filled apple with a swirl of the meringue mixture and sprinkle the almonds on top. Bake for 20 minutes, then cover with foil and bake for another 10 minutes. Dust with icing sugar and serve at once.

- *Per serving: calories 180, fat low, saturated fat low, protein low, fibre high, sodium low*

Lemony crêpes

- Total time: 30 minutes
- Budget ● Serves 4

100 g/4 oz plain flour
pinch of salt
1 egg, beaten
300 ml/½ pint milk
vegetable oil, for frying
50 g/2 oz butter
25 g/1 oz caster sugar
pared rind and juice 1 orange
100 g/4 oz lemon curd
2 tablespoons brandy (optional)

❶ Sift the flour and salt into a bowl, add the egg and beat well. Gradually beat in the milk to make a smooth batter.

❷ Heat a little of the oil in a frying pan and pour in enough batter to thinly coat the base of the pan. Cook for 1–2 minutes, turn and cook until golden. Repeat with remaining batter to make eight pancakes.

❸ Melt the butter in the pan. Remove from the heat and add the sugar, orange rind and juice; heat gently to dissolve sugar.

❹ Spread the lemon curd on the pancakes, then fold each pancake in half and half again to form a fan shape. Place the pancakes in the pan in overlapping lines and heat gently for 1–2 minutes. Warm the brandy, if using, then pour over the pancakes and set alight. Shake and serve.

- *Per serving: calories 382, fat medium, saturated fat high, protein low, fibre low, sodium medium*

Pineapple custard brûlée

- **Total time: 15 minutes**
- **Cheap** ● **Serves 4**

---

400 g/14 oz can pineapple chunks in natural juice, drained

2 tablespoons dark rum (optional)

---

100 g/4 oz thick Greek yogurt

150 ml/¼ pint ready-made pouring custard

---

1 teaspoon finely grated lemon rind

---

4 tablespoons demerara sugar

1 Divide the pineapple among four ramekin dishes and sprinkle over the rum, if using. Mix together the yogurt, custard and lemon rind and spread over the pineapple to cover completely. Sprinkle the sugar on top and grill until bubbling. Serve at once or chill until ready to serve.

● *Per serving: calories 185, fat low, saturated fat medium, protein low, fibre medium, sodium low*

Apricot upside-down tart

- **Total time: 40 minutes**
- **Budget** ● **Serves 4–6**

8–9 ripe apricots
50 g/2 oz butter
50 g/2 oz sugar
2 tablespoons double cream
1 tablespoon brandy (optional)
175 g/6 oz ready-made shortcrust pastry
vanilla ice-cream, to serve

1 Preheat the oven to 200°C/400°F/Gas 6. Place the apricots in a pan of boiling water for 1 minute, remove, plunge into cold water and peel away the skins. Cut into halves and remove the stones. Melt the butter with the sugar in a small pan. Bring to the boil and simmer for 3–4 minutes, beating continuously until thick and smooth.

2 Remove from heat, leave to cool for 1 minute, then stir in cream, beating until smooth. Spoon into a shallow 20 cm/8 in sandwich tin. Arrange the apricots on top, cut side up, and drizzle over the brandy.

3 Roll out pastry to 25 cm/10 in round. Place over apricots, pushing edges down side of tin; trim off excess pastry. Place on baking sheet and bake for 20 minutes or until pastry is golden brown. Loosen pastry from tin with knife. Cool, then turn out onto a heatproof dish and grill for 2–3 minutes until caramelised. Serve with ice-cream.

● *Per serving: calories 384, fat high, saturated fat medium, protein low, fibre medium, sodium medium*

Gooseberry fool with honey crisps

- Total time: 30 minutes
- Budget ● Serves 4

450 g/1 lb gooseberries	FOR THE HONEY CRISPS
100 g/4 oz sugar	50 g/2 oz butter
150 ml/¼ pint canned or fresh pouring custard	25 g/1 oz caster sugar
	1 small egg yolk
150 ml/¼ pint whipping cream	1 tablespoon clear honey
toasted almonds and mint sprigs, to decorate	few drops almond essence
	75 g/3 oz self-raising flour
	25 g/1 oz chopped almonds

① Preheat the oven to 190°C/375°F/Gas 5. Make the honey crisps: cream the butter and sugar. Beat in the egg yolk, honey and almond essence, then add the flour. Roll into a log shape, cut into 24 discs and place on baking sheets. Scatter with almonds and bake for 15–20 minutes; cool on a wire rack.

② Cook the gooseberries, sugar and two tablespoons water for 10–15 minutes, then pass through a fine sieve. Beat the custard into the pulp; cool a little.

③ Whip the cream until stiff and swirl into the purée. Decorate with toasted almonds and mint sprigs and serve with the crisps.

● *Per serving: calories 562, fat high, saturated fat high, protein low, fibre medium, sodium low*

Cappuccino creams

- **Total time: 20 minutes**
- **Cheap ● Serves 4**

2 teaspoons instant coffee	**300 ml/½ pint fromage frais**
2 tablespoons cream liqueur, sweet sherry or Tia Maria	**100 g/4 oz chocolate ginger biscuits, roughly crushed**
300 ml/½ pint whipping cream	**milk and white chocolate**
25 g/1 oz golden caster sugar	**shavings, to decorate**

1 Mix the coffee in a small cup with the cream liqueur, sweet sherry or Tia Maria. Pour the whipping cream into a large bowl, add the caster sugar and whip the cream until it is just beginning to hold its shape. Fold in the fromage frais and the coffee mixture.

2 Divide the crushed biscuits in half and place half in the base of four stemmed glasses. Cover the biscuit layer with half of the cream mixture. Sprinkle over the remaining biscuits and top with the rest of the cream mixture. Decorate with the chocolate shavings and chill in the fridge until ready to serve.

● *Per serving: calories 530, fat high, saturated fat high, protein low, fibre low, sodium low*

Banana fritters

- Total time: 20 minutes
- Budget • Serves 4

100 g/4 oz plain flour	oil, for deep-frying
pinch of salt	4 medium bananas, cut into
2 tablespoons icing sugar	chunks
1 egg, lightly beaten	caster sugar, for sprinkling
150 ml/¼ pint milk	

1 Sift the flour, salt and icing sugar into a bowl and make a well in the centre. Beat in the egg, then gradually beat in the milk to make a smooth batter.

2 Heat the oil in a deep-fryer to 190°C/375°F. Dip the banana chunks in the batter and deep-fry in batches for about 3 minutes until golden.

3 Drain the fritters on kitchen paper and keep warm while frying the remainder. Serve hot sprinkled with caster sugar.

• *Per serving: calories 392, fat medium, saturated fat low, protein low, fibre medium, sodium medium*

INDEX

INDEX

INDEX